Study Guide for Decoding Fahrenheit 451

With Typical Questions and Answers

Steven Smith

Sherwood Press

CONTENTS

How to use this guide

This analysis of Fahrenheit 451 intends to offer a study guide to readers who need a more in-depth view of the story.

This book is divided into questions, so the answers appear in a short essay style and may include repeated information. The questions are typical of what a middle-school or early-high-school student may experience.

I think all important questions have been directly or indirectly answered. However, if you, the reader, feel something is missing, please reach out to me, and I will add it!

Happy studying!
Steven Smith
stevensmithvo@gmail.com
www.classicbooksexplained.com

Quick Overview of Fahrenheit 451

"Fahrenheit 451" is a compelling and thought-provoking novel by Ray Bradbury, first published in 1953. This work is often considered a masterpiece of science fiction and dystopian literature, and it offers a powerful commentary on the dangers of censorship and the suppression of ideas. Here's an in-depth look at various aspects of the novel:

Plot Overview

- **Setting**: The novel is set in an unspecified city in a future society where books are banned and 'firemen' burn any that are found.

- **Main Character**: The protagonist, Guy Montag, is one of these firemen who begins to question the world around him.

- **Key Events**: The narrative follows Montag's transformation from a loyal servant of the state to a passionate advocate for intellectual freedom, spurred by encounters with his young neighbor Clarisse, his wife Mildred's overdose, and the burning of an old woman with her books.

Themes

1. Censorship:

- Central to the novel is the theme of censorship, depicted through the banning and burning of books.

- Bradbury explores how censorship limits the ability to think critically and independently, as seen in Montag's awakening.

2. The Role of Technology:

- The novel depicts technology, such as wall-sized televisions and 'seashell' earbuds, as tools for mass distraction and conformity.

- Bradbury critiques how technology can hinder meaningful communication and understanding, as illustrated by Mildred's addiction to her 'parlor walls.'

Characters

- **Guy Montag**: A fireman who evolves from a book burner to a seeker of knowledge and truth.

- **Clarisse McClellan**: A young neighbor who opens Montag's eyes to the beauty of the world and the joy of conversation.

- **Mildred Montag**: Montag's wife, deeply immersed in the shallow entertainments provided by their society.

Symbolism

- **Fire**: Traditionally a symbol of knowledge and enlightenment, fire in this novel is twisted to represent destruction and oppression.

- **The Phoenix**: Mentioned in the novel, it symbolizes rebirth and renewal, paralleling Montag's transformation.

Literary Significance and Criticism

- Bradbury's use of vivid imagery, metaphor, and allegory in "Fahrenheit 451" enriches the narrative, making it a staple in discussions about dystopian fiction.

- The novel is praised for its prescient commentary on the impact of technology and media on society, a topic that remains relevant.

Conclusion

"Fahrenheit 451" is not just a story about censorship; it's a warning about the erosion of critical thinking in the face of overwhelming media and technology. Bradbury masterfully weaves a tale that is as haunting as it is enlightening, reminding us of the enduring power of literature and the human spirit's resilience. As Montag learns, the flame of knowledge, once ignited, is difficult to extinguish. This novel stands as a beacon, urging readers to look beyond the superficial and seek the profound truths hidden in the pages of our own world's literature.

About Ray Bradbury

Ray Bradbury, the author of "Fahrenheit 451," was a prolific and influential American writer known for his imaginative and often prophetic works in the genres of science fiction, fantasy, and horror. Born on August 22, 1920, in Waukegan, Illinois, Bradbury's career spanned over seven decades, during which he wrote hundreds of short stories, numerous novels, plays, screenplays, and even poetry. Here are some key aspects of his life and work:

Early Life and Influences

- **Childhood**: Bradbury's childhood was marked by an avid interest in literature, especially fantasy and science fiction. He was a voracious reader of authors like Edgar Allan Poe, H.G. Wells, and Jules Verne.

- **Inspirations**: The early 20th-century technological advancements and the Golden Age of Radio significantly influenced his imaginative landscape.

Literary Career

- **Early Works**: Bradbury began his writing career by contributing stories to science fiction and fantasy magazines in the early 1940s.

- **Breakthrough**: His breakthrough came with the publication of

"The Martian Chronicles" (1950), a series of interrelated stories about the colonization of Mars.

- **Diverse Writing**: While best known for his science fiction works, Bradbury's writing is not easily pigeonholed; it often blends elements of fantasy, horror, and mystery.

"Fahrenheit 451"

- **Context**: Written during the McCarthy era, "Fahrenheit 451" reflects Bradbury's concerns about censorship and the stifling effect of McCarthyism.

- **Legacy**: The novel remains one of his most acclaimed works, often cited for its prescient commentary on issues like censorship, the role of technology, and the importance of literature.

Themes and Style

- **Recurring Themes**: Bradbury frequently explored themes like the conflict between technology and nature, the dangers of censorship, and the importance of imagination and creativity.

- **Style**: Known for his poetic style, Bradbury's writing is characterized by lyrical prose, vivid imagery, and a sense of wonder.

Impact and Legacy

- **Influence on Genre**: Bradbury is credited with elevating science fiction to a more serious literary genre.

- **Awards and Honors**: He received numerous awards, including the National Medal of Arts and the Pulitzer Prize Special Citation.

- **Continued Relevance**: Bradbury's works, particularly "Fahrenheit 451," continue to be relevant and are widely taught in schools.

Conclusion

Ray Bradbury's contribution to literature goes beyond genre boundaries. His ability to weave profound social and moral issues into enthralling narratives has left an indelible mark on American literature. Through works like "Fahrenheit 451," Bradbury not only entertained readers but also prompted them to reflect on critical societal issues, making his legacy both timeless and extraordinarily relevant in the modern world.

LITERARY TECHNIQUES

Ray Bradbury's "Fahrenheit 451" is a masterful work that employs various literary techniques to enhance its storytelling and thematic depth. These techniques are integral to the novel's ability to engage readers and convey its messages about censorship, technology, and the human condition. Here's an exploration of some key literary techniques used in the novel:

1. **Symbolism**:

   - Bradbury uses symbolism extensively to imbue the narrative with deeper meanings. Key symbols include books (representing knowledge and diversity of thought), the Mechanical Hound (symbolizing technological control and oppression), and fire (which has a dual symbolism of destruction and rebirth).

   - **Example**: The Phoenix, which symbolizes renewal and cyclicality, represents the potential for society to rebuild and learn from its past mistakes.

2. **Imagery**:

   - The novel is rich in vivid and evocative imagery that enhances the reader's sensory experience. This technique paints a picture of the dystopian world and underscores the novel's themes.

- **Example**: The description of the burning books creates powerful visual imagery, "The books leapt and danced like roasted birds, their wings ablaze with red and yellow feathers" (Bradbury, Part One).

3. Foreshadowing:

- Bradbury employs foreshadowing to hint at future events and to build suspense. This technique helps to keep readers engaged and to deepen the narrative's sense of foreboding.

- **Example**: Montag's encounter with his neighbor Clarisse, who questions their society's happiness, foreshadows his growing doubts and eventual rebellion.

4. Irony:

- The novel makes use of irony, particularly situational irony, to highlight the contradictions within its dystopian society.

- **Example**: The firemen in the novel, traditionally seen as figures who extinguish fires, are ironically tasked with starting fires to burn books, reflecting the perversion of societal roles in this dystopian world.

5. Allusions:

- Allusions to historical, literary, and cultural references are prevalent in the novel, adding layers of meaning and connecting the novel's themes to broader human experiences.

- **Example**: References to authors and literary works throughout the novel, such as the mention of "Dover Beach" by Matthew Arnold, enrich the story with a sense of the literary heritage that is at risk in this society.

6. **Motifs**:

○ Recurring motifs are used to reinforce the novel's central themes. These include references to fire and burning, the pervasive presence of technology, and the motif of blindness versus sight, representing ignorance and enlightenment.

○ **Example**: The image of Montag's "burning" guilt and discomfort is a recurring motif that symbolizes his growing internal conflict.

7. **Allegory**:

○ The entire novel can be read as an allegory for the dangers of censorship and the suppression of dissenting ideas. It warns against the potential consequences of state control over information and the loss of individual freedoms.

○ **Example**: The society's destruction of books and suppression of intellectualism allegorically represents historical and contemporary instances of censorship and cultural decline.

8. **Dystopian Setting**:

○ The creation of a dystopian future world is a significant literary technique in itself. It serves as a backdrop against which the themes of censorship, loss of individuality, and the effects of technology on society are explored.

○ **Example**: The depiction of a future American society obsessed with media consumption and devoid of intellectual curiosity sets the stage for the novel's exploration of its themes.

In conclusion, Bradbury's use of these literary techniques in "Fahrenheit 451" effectively communicates the novel's themes and messages, making it a compelling and thought-provoking read. The integration of symbolism, imagery, foreshadowing, irony, allusions, motifs, allegory, and dystopian elements work together to create a rich and layered narrative that continues to resonate with readers.

Why Students Study This Novel

"Fahrenheit 451" by Ray Bradbury is a staple in high school literature curricula for several compelling reasons. Its study offers students not only a gateway into classic dystopian literature but also a platform to explore a range of pertinent themes and literary techniques. Here's why it's an important novel for students to study:

1. **Understanding Dystopian Literature**:

   ○ **Definition and Features**: The novel is a quintessential example of dystopian fiction, a genre that explores a future society characterized by oppressive control and the illusion of a perfect society.

   ○ **Contextual Learning**: Students learn to compare Bradbury's vision with other dystopian works and contemporary society, fostering critical thinking about the direction of human progress.

2. **Themes Relevant to Modern Society**:

   ○ **Censorship and Freedom of Thought**: In an age where information is abundant yet often contested, studying the book's portrayal of censorship helps students understand the value of intellectual freedom and diverse perspectives.

- **Technology and Media**: Bradbury's prescient views on technology's impact on human relationships and society resonate with today's digital and media-saturated culture.

3. **Literary Analysis Skills**:

- **Symbolism and Metaphor**: The novel is rich in symbolic elements like fire and the Phoenix, providing ample material for students to analyze and interpret.

- **Bradbury's Writing Style**: His distinctive use of language, imagery, and allegory offers students a chance to explore sophisticated literary techniques.

4. **Character Development and Moral Questions**:

- **Complex Characters**: Analyzing the transformation of Guy Montag and other characters helps students understand dynamic character development and its role in driving narrative.

- **Ethical and Philosophical Discussions**: The moral dilemmas and philosophical questions posed in the novel encourage deep, reflective thinking and discussions among students.

5. **Cultural and Historical Context**:

- **Cold War Era Reflections**: Understanding the book's context — the McCarthy era and the Cold War — aids students in grasping the historical influences on literary works.

- **Enduring Relevance**: Discussing the novel's continued relevance helps students connect historical events to current issues, enhancing their historical and cultural awareness.

6. **Encouraging a Love for Literature**:

- ○ **Appreciation of Books and Reading**: At its heart, "Fahrenheit 451" is a celebration of literature and its role in human understanding, inspiring students to value and engage with literary works.

Conclusion

Studying "Fahrenheit 451" equips students with critical thinking skills and a nuanced understanding of complex themes, making it an invaluable part of the high school curriculum. The novel's exploration of censorship, the role of technology, and the power of literature offers a timeless lesson on the importance of preserving and understanding diverse viewpoints in a rapidly changing world.

Understanding Dystopian Literature

Expanding on the first reason why students study "Fahrenheit 451" — understanding dystopian literature — involves going deeper into the definition of the genre, its features, and the importance of contextual learning:

1. **Definition and Characteristics of Dystopian Literature**:

   ○ **Dystopia Defined**: Dystopian literature presents an imagined future society that is deceptively ideal or significantly worse than the present. It often serves as a cautionary tale.

   ○ **Key Features**:

     • **Authoritarian Governance**: Dystopias frequently feature oppressive government regimes or societal structures that exert control over individuals, often under the guise of a utopian society.

     • **Loss of Individuality**: These societies typically suppress individuality and freedom, prioritizing conformity and the collective over personal identity and autonomy.

     • **Surveillance and Propaganda**: The use of surveillance, propaganda, and manipulation of information is common, maintaining control over the populace.

     • **Themes of Rebellion and Resistance**: Central to many

dystopian narratives is the theme of resistance or rebellion against the oppressive system, as seen through the protagonist's journey.

2. Contextual Learning Through "Fahrenheit 451":

- **Connection to Historical Contexts**: Bradbury's novel, written during the McCarthy era, reflects the paranoia and fear of censorship and suppression of dissenting ideas prevalent at that time. This connection helps students understand how historical events can influence literature.

- **Contemporary Relevance**: By examining "Fahrenheit 451" in the context of modern society, students can draw parallels between the novel's themes and current global issues, such as government surveillance, the impact of technology on human interaction, and the manipulation of information in media.

- **Comparative Analysis**: Students can compare "Fahrenheit 451" with other dystopian works like George Orwell's "1984" or Aldous Huxley's "Brave New World," analyzing similarities and differences in how these narratives address themes like control, resistance, and the human spirit. This comparative approach deepens their understanding of the genre as a whole.

Conclusion

Studying "Fahrenheit 451" provides students with a foundational understanding of dystopian literature, its characteristics, and its significance. It enables them to recognize the genre's role in critiquing societal trends and highlighting the potential consequences of certain paths of progress.

Through this novel, students learn to appreciate the power of literature as a reflective and predictive tool, offering insights into both the time it was written and the future it envisions.

Themes Relevant to Modern Society

Expanding on the second reason why students study "Fahrenheit 451" — the exploration of themes relevant to modern society — involves a deeper look at how the novel's themes of censorship, freedom of thought, technology, and media impact and resonate with contemporary audiences:

Censorship and Freedom of Thought:

1. **Censorship in the Novel**: "Fahrenheit 451" portrays a society where books are banned and critical thinking is suppressed, highlighting the dangers of censorship.

2. **Relevance Today**: In an era where issues of free speech, "fake news," and the control of information are hotly debated, the novel's exploration of these themes remains strikingly relevant. It prompts students to consider the importance of safeguarding intellectual freedom and diverse viewpoints in maintaining a healthy, democratic society.

3. **Critical Thinking and Diversity of Ideas**: Bradbury's narrative encourages students to value diverse perspectives and to think critically about the information they receive. This is particularly important in an educational context where fostering independent thought and respect for different ideas is key.

Technology and Media:

1. **Technological Control in the Novel**: The novel presents technology, particularly the immersive and interactive 'parlor walls,' as tools for distraction and indoctrination, diminishing the value placed on human experience and genuine relationships.

2. **Current Context**: In today's digital age, where technology and media are integral to daily life, students can draw parallels to the novel's depiction of technology's potential to isolate individuals and control public opinion.

3. **Discussion on Media Consumption**: "Fahrenheit 451" opens up discussions about the impact of social media, the internet, and digital devices on human behavior and society. It challenges students to reflect on their own media consumption habits and the potential effects of technology on mental health, social interactions, and the dissemination of information.

Conclusion

Through its exploration of censorship, freedom of thought, and the role of technology and media, "Fahrenheit 451" serves as a powerful tool for students to understand and critique these issues in the context of their own lives and society. Bradbury's foresight in addressing these themes makes the novel an enduring and relevant piece of literature, offering valuable lessons about the preservation of individuality, critical thinking, and the responsible use of technology in an increasingly complex world.

LITERARY ANALYSIS SKILLS

Looking deeper into the third reason why students study "Fahrenheit 451" — the development of literary analysis skills — involves exploring how the novel's use of symbolism, metaphor, and Bradbury's distinctive writing style serve as excellent resources for honing critical reading and analytical skills:

1. **Symbolism and Metaphor**:

   - **Fire as a Symbol**: In "Fahrenheit 451," fire represents both destruction and enlightenment. Initially, it symbolizes the destructive power of censorship, but as the story progresses, it also comes to represent knowledge and enlightenment, particularly in the context of Montag's awakening.

   - **The Phoenix**: The Phoenix, which is mentioned in the novel, symbolizes rebirth and renewal. It parallels Montag's transformation and the hope for a society that learns from its past.

   - **The Mechanical Hound**: Symbolizing government control and the suppression of dissent, the Mechanical Hound is a metaphor for the dehumanizing effects of technology and authoritarianism.

   - **Analyzing Symbolism**: Students learn to identify and interpret these symbols, understanding how they contribute to the themes and overall message of the novel.

2. Bradbury's Writing Style:

- **Language and Imagery**: Bradbury's use of rich, descriptive language and vivid imagery creates a distinct atmosphere and evokes strong emotional responses. Analyzing his style helps students appreciate the power of language in storytelling.

- **Allegory and Allusions**: The novel is replete with allegorical elements and allusions to other literary works and historical events. Understanding these references enhances students' comprehension of the text and its broader implications.

- **Narrative Structure**: Examining the structure of the novel, including its pacing, point of view, and the development of tension, allows students to understand how these elements contribute to the effectiveness of storytelling.

3. Critical Thinking and Interpretation:

- **Thematic Analysis**: Students engage in thematic analysis, exploring how themes are developed through characters, settings, and plot. This encourages deeper engagement with the text and its underlying messages.

- **Discussion and Debate**: The novel's complex themes and moral questions provide ample material for classroom discussion and debate, fostering students' ability to articulate and defend their interpretations and viewpoints.

Conclusion

Studying "Fahrenheit 451" enhances students' literary analysis skills by providing them with a rich text full of symbolic and metaphorical content, as well as a unique narrative style to dissect and interpret. This process not only deepens their understanding of Bradbury's work but also equips them with critical thinking skills that are applicable across various literary genres and in broader academic and real-world contexts.

Character Development and Moral Questions

Expanding on the fourth reason why students study "Fahrenheit 451" — the exploration of character development and moral questions — involves looking closely at how the novel's characters evolve and the ethical dilemmas they face, which offer profound lessons and encourage deep reflection:

1. **Character Development**:

   - **Guy Montag's Transformation**: Montag's journey from a complacent fireman to a questioning rebel provides a rich study in character development. Analyzing his evolution helps students understand how characters can embody a narrative's themes and moral questions.

   - **Influence of Secondary Characters**: Characters like Clarisse McClellan and Captain Beatty play crucial roles in Montag's transformation. Exploring these dynamics allows students to appreciate how interactions between characters can drive plot and theme development.

2. **Moral and Ethical Questions**:

   - **The Ethics of Censorship**: The novel raises critical questions about the morality of censorship and its impact on society. Students are prompted to consider when, if ever, censorship might be justified.

- **The Value of Knowledge and Literature**: Bradbury's work provokes thought on the intrinsic value of knowledge and literature in human life, encouraging students to reflect on why societies should preserve these treasures.

- **Conformity vs. Individuality**: The tension between societal conformity and individual thought in the novel serves as a platform for discussion about the importance of individuality and personal freedom.

3. **Philosophical and Societal Reflections**:

- **Impact of Technology on Humanity**: The novel's portrayal of a society obsessed with technology, at the expense of intellectual and emotional depth, raises questions about the role and impact of technology in our own lives.

- **Responsibility to Society and Self**: Montag's struggle represents a broader philosophical debate about the individual's responsibility to oneself versus society, a pertinent issue for young adults navigating their roles in their communities.

4. **Critical Thinking and Empathy**:

- **Understanding Complex Characters**: By analyzing characters who are not clearly "good" or "evil," students develop a nuanced understanding of human behavior and motivations.

- **Empathetic Engagement**: Engaging with the characters' struggles and transformations fosters empathy and a deeper understanding of the human condition.

Conclusion

Through its rich character development and exploration of moral and ethical questions, "Fahrenheit 451" serves as a vital tool for students in understanding complex human behaviors and societal issues. The novel not only enhances their analytical and empathetic skills but also encourages them to grapple with important philosophical questions, preparing them to engage thoughtfully with the world around them.

Cultural and Historical Context

Expanding on the fifth reason why students study "Fahrenheit 451" — understanding the cultural and historical context of the novel — involves exploring how the book reflects its time of creation and offers timeless insights into human society and behavior:

1. **Reflection of the Historical Context**:

   ○ **McCarthy Era and Cold War Influences**: "Fahrenheit 451" was written during the McCarthy era, a time marked by intense anti-communist sentiment and censorship in the United States. Understanding this context helps students see how the novel reflects the paranoia and fear of intellectual suppression prevalent during the 1950s.

   ○ **Technological Advancements**: The novel also mirrors the rapid technological advancements of the time, particularly in the field of television and mass media, and their potential impact on society.

2. **Enduring Relevance**:

   ○ **Timeless Themes**: Despite its specific historical context, "Fahrenheit 451" addresses themes like censorship, the role of technology, and the importance of critical thinking, which remain relevant in today's society.

○ **Modern Parallels**: Students can draw parallels between the novel's portrayal of a controlled, complacent society and contemporary issues such as the influence of technology on our lives, the manipulation of information, and challenges to free speech.

3. **Cultural Significance**:

○ **Influence on Literature and Media**: The novel has significantly impacted literature and popular culture, influencing various works and media forms that explore similar themes.

○ **Role in Public Discourse**: "Fahrenheit 451" is often cited in discussions about censorship and freedom of expression, highlighting its role in shaping public discourse on these critical issues.

4. **Broader Historical Awareness**:

○ **Connection to Other Historical Movements**: By placing "Fahrenheit 451" in a broader historical context, students can connect it to other literary movements and historical events, enriching their understanding of the continuous interplay between history and literature.

○ **Critical Analysis of Historical Influence**: Students learn to critically analyze how historical contexts influence literary themes and styles, enhancing their ability to interpret and understand literature in relation to its time.

Conclusion

Studying "Fahrenheit 451" in its cultural and historical context gives students a deeper understanding of how literature reflects and influences the society in which it is created. The novel serves as a bridge between past and present, allowing students to appreciate the enduring power of literature to comment on and shape human thought and societal trends. This understanding is crucial in helping them become well-rounded, historically informed individuals.

Encouraging a Love for Literature

Expanding on the sixth reason why students study "Fahrenheit 451" — encouraging a love for literature — involves exploring how Ray Bradbury's novel fosters an appreciation for reading and understanding the power of literary works:

1. **Celebration of Literature and Knowledge**:

   - **Intrinsic Value of Books**: "Fahrenheit 451" highlights the importance of books as vessels of knowledge, culture, and diverse ideas. The narrative emphasizes that literature is essential for personal growth and societal well-being.

   - **Contrast with a Bookless Society**: The dystopian setting, where books are banned and critical thinking is discouraged, serves as a stark reminder of the richness that literature brings to our lives.

2. **Critical Engagement with Texts**:

   - **Active Reading Skills**: The novel challenges students to engage actively with the text, interpreting symbolism, themes, and character development. This process fosters a deeper appreciation of the complexities and rewards of reading.

   - **Discussion and Analysis**: Classroom discussions about the novel encourage students to articulate their thoughts and in-

terpretations, enhancing their analytical skills and their ability
to appreciate different perspectives.

3. Understanding the Power of Words:

- **Influence of Language**: Bradbury's masterful use of language, with its vivid imagery and compelling narrative style, demonstrates the power of words to evoke emotions, provoke thought, and create immersive worlds.

- **Literature as a Tool for Change**: The novel exemplifies how literature can be a powerful tool for reflection, resistance, and change, inspiring students to view reading and writing as meaningful and impactful activities.

4. Connecting with Universal Themes:

- **Human Experience and Emotions**: "Fahrenheit 451" touches on universal themes such as freedom, conformity, and the quest for meaning, allowing students to connect with the text on a personal level.

- **Empathy and Understanding**: Through the characters' experiences, students develop empathy and a deeper understanding of the human condition, fostering a love for stories that explore these aspects of life.

5. Lifelong Learning and Curiosity:

- **Inspiring Curiosity**: The novel encourages students to be curious about the world around them, to question and to seek out knowledge, traits that are fundamental to a lifelong love of learning.

- **Gateway to Other Literary Works**: Studying "Fahrenheit 451" can serve as a gateway to exploring other literary works, genres, and authors, broadening students' literary horizons.

Conclusion

In studying "Fahrenheit 451," students gain an appreciation for Bradbury's skill as a writer and the profound impact literature can have on individuals and society. The novel serves as a powerful reminder of why literature matters, inspiring a love for reading and an understanding of the transformative power of the written word.

CHAPTER POINT-FORM SUMMARY

The book is divided into three parts, each with its own chapters and significant developments.

Part One: The Hearth and the Salamander

Chapter 1:

- **Introduction to Guy Montag**: The novel opens with Guy Montag, a fireman who burns books for a living in a futuristic American city. In this society, firemen start fires rather than put them out.

- **Montag's Encounter with Clarisse**: Montag meets his new neighbor, Clarisse McClellan, a seventeen-year-old girl who introduces him to a world of ideas, contemplative thought, and natural beauty that he never knew existed.

- **Montag's Growing Discontent**: Through Clarisse's questions and conversations, Montag becomes aware of his unhappiness and begins questioning the world around him.

Chapter 2:

- **Montag's Changing Perspective**: Montag continues interacting with Clarisse over the next few days. Her curiosity and love for life starkly contrast with his wife Mildred's shallow existence, absorbed by the television and indifferent to Montag's growing concern.

- **Mildred's Overdose**: Montag discovers that Mildred has overdosed on sleeping pills. After the emergency crew revives her, she seems oblivious to the near-death experience, further alienating Montag.

- **Montag's Secret**: It's revealed that Montag has been secretly hiding books in his house, an act of rebellion against the anti-intellectual norms of his society.

Part Two: The Sieve and the Sand

Chapter 1:
- **Montag's Crisis of Faith**: Montag becomes increasingly disillusioned with his role as a fireman and the society's censorship of books.

- **Encounter with Captain Beatty**: Captain Beatty, Montag's boss, visits him. Beatty explains the history of censorship and the firemen, arguing that books are dangerous as they contain conflicting ideas that can lead to discontent and unhappiness.

Chapter 2:
- **Montag Seeks Help**: Montag turns to Professor Faber, a former English professor he had met previously, for guidance. Faber explains the value of literature and helps Montag devise a plan to fight against the book-burning regime.

- **The Plan**: They plan to plant books in the homes of firemen to discredit the profession and the anti-book culture.

Chapter 3:

- **Montag's Reading**: Montag attempts to read the books he has hoarded to find the meaning they might contain. He struggles to understand and retain the information, likened metaphorically to trying to fill a sieve with sand.

- **Conflict with Mildred**: Montag's wife, Mildred, is uncomfortable and fearful of the books. The tension between them grows as Montag's disillusionment with society increases.

- **Montag's Plan with Faber**: Montag and Faber finalize their plan. Faber provides Montag with a two-way radio earpiece (the "green bullet") so they can communicate secretly.

Part Three: Burning Bright

Chapter 1:

- **Montag's Confrontation with Beatty**: Montag's transformation becomes evident when he is called to burn a house and discovers it's his own. Aware of Montag's rebellion, Captain Beatty forces Montag to burn his house with a flamethrower.

- **Montag's Drastic Action**: In a climactic moment, Montag turns the flamethrower on Beatty, killing him and becoming a fugitive.

- **The Mechanical Hound**: Montag is pursued by the Mechanical Hound, a robotic enforcer used by the firemen. He narrowly escapes after injuring the Hound.

Chapter 2:

- **On the Run**: Montag flees the city, pursued by the authorities. He realizes the depth of his alienation from society and the extent of the state's control over individuals.

- **Encounter with the Book People**: Montag finds a group of rebels living in the countryside. These individuals, led by a man named Granger, have each memorized a book to preserve its contents from the anti-intellectual regime.

- **Montag's New Purpose**: Montag learns that the rebels are part of a larger network of book lovers who hope to rebuild society with the knowledge preserved in their memories.

Chapter 3:
- **Destruction and Hope**: As war ravages the city, Montag and his new companions witness the destruction from afar. The novel ends with a sense of hope, as Montag and the group move towards the ruins to help rebuild civilization, armed with the knowledge they carry within them.

Analytical Insights:

- **Montag's Journey**: Montag's transformation from a conformist fireman to a questioning rebel is central to the novel's exploration of themes such as censorship, the power of knowledge, and individuality versus conformity.

- **Society's Downfall**: The novel's climax, with the destruction of the city, serves as a powerful metaphor for the self-destructive nature of a society that refuses to embrace diversity of thought and suppresses intellectual freedom.

- **Preservation of Knowledge**: The role of the Book People highlights the importance of literature and knowledge in maintaining the fabric of society. Their commitment to memorizing books symbolizes the resilience of human culture and the power of the individual in the face of oppressive regimes.

Chapter Summary

Part One: The Hearth and the Salamander

Chapter 1: The Encounter

In the cold grip of a future society, we meet Guy Montag, whose profession as a fireman entails igniting, not extinguishing, the forbidden fruit of knowledge – books. Amidst the flames, his existence is unshaken until he encounters Clarisse McClellan. This young neighbor, with her peculiar curiosity and vivacious spirit, unveils before Montag a world he never perceived – one where the beauty of nature, the joy of conversation, and the depths of observation matter.

Chapter 2: The Awakening

As Montag's interactions with Clarisse continue, a seed of doubt takes root in his mind. Contrasting Clarisse's reflective nature with his wife Mildred's immersion in the superficial entertainment of their society, Montag becomes conscious of a profound emptiness within himself and the world around him. This realization is further amplified when he discovers Mildred's unconscious form, a victim to an overdose of sleeping pills, a symbol of society's numbing indifference.

Part Two: The Sieve and the Sand

Chapter 1: The Questioning

Montag, now a cauldron of internal conflict, grapples with the principles of his society. Captain Beatty, sensing Montag's dissent, pays him a visit. Beatty, a cunning orator, recounts the history and the justification for their book-burning society, emphasizing the perceived happiness gleaned from conformity and intellectual uniformity.

Chapter 2: The Rebellion

In a desperate quest for understanding, Montag turns to a forbidden trove – his secret cache of books. Struggling to decipher their meaning, he seeks the aid of Professor Faber, an outcast from the world of academia. Together, they hatch a perilous plan to upend the societal disdain for literature by planting books in the homes of unsuspecting firemen, thereby sowing the seeds of doubt and dissent.

Part Three: Burning Bright

Chapter 1: The Conflagration

Montag's rebellion reaches a fever pitch when he is commanded to incinerate his own abode. In a defiant blaze, he turns his flamethrower upon Captain Beatty, thus severing his ties with the regime he once served. Pursued by the Mechanical Hound, a symbol of the state's relentless control, Montag narrowly escapes into the wilderness.

Chapter 2: The Fugitive

As a fugitive, Montag encounters a band of societal outcasts – the 'Book People.' These individuals, each having memorized a book, represent the enduring resilience of knowledge. Montag, now an apostle of their cause, joins them in their mission to preserve the written word.

Chapter 3: The Phoenix

As war ravages the city, Montag and his newfound companions witness its destruction from afar. In the ashes of the fallen society, they find hope – a chance to rebuild from the ruins, armed with the immutable power of knowledge and literature.

Part One Summary

In the first part of Ray Bradbury's "Fahrenheit 451," titled "The Hearth and the Salamander," the narrative unfolds in a chronologically linear fashion, introducing us to the protagonist, Guy Montag, and his journey from complacency to a burgeoning awareness of the stifling nature of his society. This section is pivotal as it lays the groundwork for the themes and conflicts that will be further explored in the subsequent parts of the novel.

Chapter 1: The Hearth and the Salamander

- **Introduction to Guy Montag**: We meet Guy Montag, a fireman in a dystopian future where books are banned and the primary duty of firemen is to burn them. Montag initially takes pride in his role, which is evident in the opening lines, "It was a pleasure to burn" (Bradbury, "Fahrenheit 451").

- **Montag's Encounter with Clarisse McClellan**: On his way home from work, Montag meets his seventeen-year-old neighbor, Clarisse McClellan. Clarisse's curious and questioning nature stands in stark contrast to the conformist society around them. She asks Montag if he is happy, a question that unsettles him and begins to ignite his journey of self-questioning.

- **Montag at Home**: Returning home, Montag is confronted with the emptiness of his life and marriage. His wife, Mildred, is obsessed with interactive television and indifferent to Montag's growing unease. Their conversation reveals the superficiality and disconnect in their relationship.

- **Mildred's Overdose**: Montag awakens to find Mildred has over-dosed on sleeping pills. This incident, treated with casual indiffer-ence by the emergency medical technicians who revive her, further illustrates the pervasive apathy of their society.

- **Montag and Clarisse's Continued Interactions**: In the follow-ing days, Montag's encounters with Clarisse continue. She intro-duces him to new experiences, like tasting the rain and observing nature, which further distance him from the numbness of his daily life.

Chapter 2: Montag's Growing Discontent

- **Montag's Reflections**: Influenced by Clarisse, Montag begins to reflect on the nature of his work and the society in which he lives. He starts questioning the purpose and morality of burning books.

- **The Mechanical Hound**: Montag interacts with the Mechanical Hound, a robotic creature used by the firemen, at the firehouse. Montag suspects that the Hound is hostile towards him, symbol-izing his growing disconnect from his job and his society.

- **Montag's Secret**: The chapter concludes with Montag revealing to the reader that he has secretly been stealing and hiding books from the houses he burns. This act of rebellion signifies the begin-ning of Montag's transformation and his quest for understanding.

Conclusion of Part One

Part One of "Fahrenheit 451" effectively sets the stage for Montag's transformation. Bradbury introduces key themes such as censorship, the dehumanizing effects of technology, and the power of individual thought. Montag's encounters with Clarisse serve as a catalyst for his growing discontent with his life and society, propelling him towards a path of self-discovery and rebellion. This section of the novel lays the foundation for the dramatic developments that follow, as Montag seeks to find meaning in a world where books and independent thinking are forbidden.

Part Two Summary

Part Two of Ray Bradbury's "Fahrenheit 451," titled "The Sieve and the Sand," delves deeper into the protagonist Guy Montag's evolving consciousness and escalating rebellion against his society's oppressive norms. This part of the novel is crucial for its exploration of themes such as the power and value of knowledge, the conflict between understanding and ignorance, and the quest for personal freedom.

Chapter 1: Montag's Crisis and Beatty's Visit

- **Montag's Internal Turmoil**: The chapter begins with Montag feeling increasingly alienated and disturbed by the society around him. His interactions with Clarisse have opened his eyes to the emptiness and shallowness of his existence. He begins to question not just his role as a fireman but the very foundations of his society.

- **Mildred's Indifference**: Montag attempts to engage Mildred in conversation about the content of the books he has secretly collected. However, she is largely indifferent and unable to comprehend the importance of what Montag is trying to convey. This further exacerbates Montag's sense of isolation.

- **Captain Beatty's Exposition**: Sensing Montag's growing dissent, Captain Beatty visits him at his home. In a lengthy monologue, Beatty explains the history of how society came to eschew books and intellectualism. He argues that books create disparities in opinion, leading to conflict and unhappiness. This exposition is crucial as it provides insight into the rationale behind the society's censorship and anti-intellectual stance.

Chapter 2: Montag's Quest for Knowledge

- **Montag's Desperation**: Feeling overwhelmed by his newfound awareness and the weight of his secret stash of books, Montag seeks guidance and comprehension. He struggles with reading the books he has accumulated, likening the experience to trying to fill a sieve with sand - a metaphor for his inability to grasp and retain the knowledge he so desperately seeks.

- **Turning to Faber**: Montag recalls an encounter with an old English professor named Faber and decides to contact him for help. Faber represents the antithesis of the society's norms - a man who values literature, understanding, and independent thought.

- **The Plan with Faber**: In a pivotal scene, Montag visits Faber, and they formulate a plan to subvert the status quo. Faber explains the importance of books, stating that it's not just the books themselves that are vital, but the meaningful content they carry. Together, they devise a strategy to plant books in the homes of firemen to discredit the profession and undermine the societal taboo against literature.

Conclusion of Part Two

In "The Sieve and the Sand," Montag's journey from a conforming fireman to a questioning rebel reaches a critical point. The interactions with Beatty and Faber serve to highlight the contrasting perspectives on the value of knowledge and the role of books in society. This part of the novel is instrumental in setting the stage for Montag's ultimate act of rebellion and the story's dramatic climax. Through Montag's internal struggles and his actions, Bradbury eloquently explores the themes of intellectual freedom, the importance of dissent in a conformist society, and the transformative power of knowledge.

Part Three Summary

Part Three of Ray Bradbury's "Fahrenheit 451," titled "Burning Bright," is the culmination of Guy Montag's transformation and his confrontation with the dystopian society that seeks to suppress knowledge and individual thought. This concluding section is pivotal, as it brings to fruition the themes of rebellion, the pursuit of knowledge, and the quest for a new beginning in the aftermath of societal collapse.

Chapter 1: Montag's Confrontation and Rebellion

- **Montag's House Burns**: The chapter opens with a shocking turn of events. Montag and his fellow firemen are called to an unknown location to burn books, only to discover that the destination is his own house. This moment is a stark realization for Montag of his complete alienation from the society he once served.

- **Beatty's Provocation**: Captain Beatty, aware of Montag's treachery, taunts him. Beatty's antagonism and his revelations about the firemen's awareness of Montag's dissent culminate in a tense standoff.

- **Montag's Drastic Response**: In a moment of crisis, Montag turns the flamethrower on Beatty, killing him. This act signifies Montag's final break with his past life and his total rejection of the oppressive society.

- **Flight from the Mechanical Hound**: Montag flees as the Mechanical Hound, a symbol of the state's oppressive power, is deployed to hunt him down. He manages to evade the Hound, but not before it injures him, marking him both physically and symbolically as an outcast.

Chapter 2: Montag's Flight and Discovery

- **Montag on the Run**: Montag, now a fugitive, takes refuge in the home of fellow fireman Black, where he plants books to implicate him, as part of the plan he devised with Faber.

- **The River Escape**: Pursued relentlessly, Montag escapes to the river. His journey down the river symbolizes a baptismal passage – a cleansing and rebirth into a new life.

- **Encounter with the 'Book People'**: Montag's flight leads him to a group of societal outcasts living on the fringes of society. Each member has committed an entire book to memory, becoming a living vessel of knowledge in a world where books are forbidden.

Chapter 3: The Phoenix's Rebirth

- **Montag's Integration**: Montag is welcomed into the group, led by a man named Granger. He learns about their mission to preserve literature and knowledge, and he is assigned a book to memorize, contributing to this legacy.

- **Destruction and Renewal**: As they watch their city be destroyed by bombs in the distance, the group remains hopeful. Granger reflects on the myth of the Phoenix, a symbol of rebirth, suggesting that humanity can learn from its past and rebuild.

- **A New Beginning**: The novel concludes with Montag and the group setting off to find survivors of the bombing, carrying with them the hope of rebuilding society. This ending encapsulates the novel's ultimate message: the enduring power of knowledge and the resilience of the human spirit.

Conclusion of Part Three

In "Burning Bright," the narrative reaches its climax, showcasing Montag's final transformation from a conformist to a rebel, and ultimately to a preserver of knowledge. This part of the novel is a powerful testament to Bradbury's themes of resistance against censorship, the importance of literature, and the potential for renewal in the face of destruction. Montag's journey is emblematic of the struggle for intellectual freedom and the quest for a better, more enlightened society. Through its dramatic conclusion, "Fahrenheit 451" leaves a lasting impression on the reader, championing the resilience of human culture and the unquenchable thirst for knowledge.

Transformation of Guy Montag

Journeying through its chapters, let's unveil the transformation of Guy Montag, a fireman in a dystopian world where books are burned to ashes.

Part One: The Hearth and the Salamander

Chapter 1: The Encounter

In the cold grip of a future society, we meet Guy Montag, whose profession as a fireman entails igniting, not extinguishing, the forbidden fruit of knowledge – books. Amidst the flames, his existence is unshaken until he encounters Clarisse McClellan. With her peculiar curiosity and vivacious spirit, this young neighbor unveils before Montag a world he never perceived – one where the beauty of nature, the joy of conversation, and the depths of observation matter.

Chapter 2: The Awakening

As Montag's interactions with Clarisse burgeon, a seed of doubt takes root in his mind. Contrasting Clarisse's reflective nature with his wife Mildred's immersion in the superficial entertainment of their society, Montag becomes conscious of a profound emptiness within himself and the world around him. This realization is further amplified when he discovers Mildred's unconscious form, a victim to an overdose of sleeping pills, a symbol of society's numbing indifference.

Part Two: The Sieve and the Sand

Chapter 1: The Questioning

Montag, now a cauldron of internal conflict, grapples with the principles of his society. Captain Beatty, sensing Montag's dissent, pays him a visit. Beatty, a cunning orator, recounts the history and the justification for their book-burning society, emphasizing the perceived happiness gleaned from conformity and intellectual uniformity.

Chapter 2: The Rebellion

In a desperate quest for understanding, Montag turns to a forbidden trove – his secret cache of books. Struggling to decipher their meaning, he seeks the aid of Professor Faber, an outcast from the world of academia. Together, they hatch a perilous plan to upend the societal disdain for literature by planting books in the homes of unsuspecting firemen, thereby sowing the seeds of doubt and dissent.

Part Three: Burning Bright

Chapter 1: The Conflagration

Montag's rebellion reaches a fever pitch when he is commanded to incinerate his own abode. In a defiant blaze, he turns his flamethrower upon Captain Beatty, thus severing his ties with the regime he once served. Pursued by the Mechanical Hound, a symbol of the state's relentless control, Montag narrowly escapes into the wilderness.

Chapter 2: The Fugitive

As a fugitive, Montag encounters a band of societal outcasts – the 'Book People.' These individuals, each having memorized a book, represent the enduring resilience of knowledge. Montag, now an apostle of their cause, joins them in their mission to preserve the written word.

Chapter 3: The Phoenix

As war ravages the city, Montag and his newfound companions witness its destruction from afar. In the ashes of the fallen society, they find hope – a chance to rebuild from the ruins, armed with the immutable power of knowledge and literature.

In this tale, Bradbury weaves a cautionary fabric, warning of a future where intellectual freedom is shackled, and the pursuit of knowledge is a perilous path. Montag's odyssey from conformity to enlightenment embodies the eternal struggle against the forces of censorship and complacency. "Fahrenheit 451" stands as a story and a beacon, illuminating the importance of preserving our ability to think, question, and dream.

THEMES

"Fahrenheit 451" is full of themes, each interwoven to create a compelling narrative that explores the consequences of censorship, the loss of individual thought, and the redemptive power of knowledge. Let us delve into these themes, highlighting key references from the novel to illustrate each.

1. Censorship and Intellectual Oppression

- **Reference**: Captain Beatty, explaining the rationale behind book burning, states, "We must all be alike. Not everyone born free and equal, as the Constitution says, but everyone made equal" (Bradbury, "Fahrenheit 451", Part One).

- **Explanation**: This theme is central to the novel's dystopian setting, where books are banned to prevent discord and maintain societal uniformity. It critiques the dangers of suppressing dissenting ideas and the resulting loss of critical thinking and creativity.

2. The Destructive Impact of Technology

- **Reference**: Mildred's immersion in the 'parlor walls' and her disconnection from reality is evident when she says, "My 'family' is people. They tell me things; I laugh, they laugh! And the colors!" (Bradbury, Part One).

- **Explanation**: Bradbury explores how an overreliance on technology can lead to a superficial existence, devoid of real human connection and introspection. The novel warns of technology's potential to distract and dull the human experience.

3. Knowledge and Human Understanding

- ○ **Reference**: Faber emphasizes the importance of books when he tells Montag, "The magic is only in what books say, how they stitched the patches of the universe together into one garment for us" (Bradbury, Part Two).

- ○ **Explanation**: This theme underscores the value of literature and knowledge as tools for understanding the world and oneself. The novel posits that the true value of books lies in their ability to enlighten and provoke thought.

4. Conformity vs. Individuality

- ○ **Reference**: Clarisse's uncle says, "If you don't want a man unhappy politically, don't give him two sides to a question to worry him; give him one. Better yet, give him none" (Bradbury, Part One).

- ○ **Explanation**: The novel presents a society that values conformity over individuality, where questioning the status quo is discouraged. It highlights the importance of individual thought in fostering a vibrant and healthy society.

5. Transformation and Redemption

- ○ **Reference**: Montag's transformation is evident when he reflects, "He was not happy. He was not happy. He said the words to himself. He recognized this as the true state of affairs"

(Bradbury, Part One).

- ○ **Explanation**: Montag's journey from a complacent fire-man to a seeker of truth exemplifies the theme of personal transformation and redemption. The novel suggests that it is never too late to challenge one's beliefs and seek a more meaningful existence.

6. The Role of Art and Culture in Society

- ○ **Reference**: Montag, reading poetry to Mildred and her friends, chooses Matthew Arnold's "Dover Beach," which reflects on the loss of faith and the erosion of human culture (Bradbury, Part Two).

- ○ **Explanation**: Through Montag's interactions with literature, the novel explores the role of art and culture in providing depth and meaning to human experience, acting as a counterbalance to a sterile, technology-driven existence.

7. Rebirth and Hope

- ○ **Reference**: The novel's ending, with Montag joining the 'Book People' and the city's destruction, suggests a cycle of destruction and rebirth, akin to the Phoenix myth mentioned in the narrative (Bradbury, Part Three).

- ○ **Explanation**: Despite its depiction of a dystopian society, the novel ends on a note of hope, suggesting the possibility of renewal and the enduring power of human resilience and knowledge.

In conclusion, "Fahrenheit 451" is a multifaceted exploration of themes relevant to both its mid-20th-century context and the present day. Bradbury's visionary narrative serves as a cautionary tale about the dangers of censorship, the dehumanizing effects of technology, and the importance of individual thought, while ultimately affirming the transformative power of knowledge and the enduring hope for a better future.

CENSORSHIP AND INTELLECTUAL OPPRESSION

The theme of censorship and intellectual oppression is a cornerstone of "Fahrenheit 451," offering a profound commentary on the consequences of suppressing dissenting ideas and the impact of such actions on society. This theme is not merely a backdrop but the very essence of the dystopian world Bradbury envisions, where the state has outlawed books and intellectual discourse. The narrative meticulously unravels how censorship is used as a tool for control, leading to a populace devoid of critical thinking and independent thought. Let's explore this theme in detail, referencing specific parts of the novel to illustrate its significance.

1. **State-Enforced Censorship**:

   ○ **Captain Beatty's Explanation**: In a pivotal conversation with Montag, Captain Beatty, the fire chief, explains the rationale behind the state's policy of book burning. He says, "We must all be alike. Not everyone born free and equal, as the Constitution says, but everyone made equal. Each man is the image of every other; then all are happy, for there are no mountains to make them cower, to judge themselves against" (Bradbury, "Fahrenheit 451", Part One). This chilling justification highlights how censorship is used to enforce conformity and suppress individuality, creating a society where intellectual sameness is equated with happiness and safety.

2. Suppression of Dissenting Ideas:

○ **Destruction of Books**: The act of burning books, the primary occupation of firemen like Guy Montag, symbolizes the literal and figurative destruction of knowledge. Early in the novel, Montag reflects with satisfaction on his role: "It was a pleasure to burn. It was a special pleasure to see things eaten, to see things blackened and changed" (Bradbury, Part One). This quote underscores the government's extreme measures to control information and reflects the indoctrination of individuals like Montag who initially do not question their actions.

3. Consequences of Intellectual Oppression:

○ **Society's Apathy and Decline**: The novel vividly portrays a society in decline, where people like Montag's wife, Mildred, are immersed in shallow entertainment and are indifferent to the world around them. Mildred's obsession with the 'parlor walls' and her emotional detachment symbolize the broader societal malaise. This is evident when Mildred nonchalantly tells Montag about her "family" in the parlor walls, displaying a profound disconnection from reality (Bradbury, Part One).

○ **Montag's Awakening**: Montag's transformation from a conformist fireman to a seeker of knowledge epitomizes the human struggle against intellectual oppression. His journey begins with a simple, yet profound question posed by Clarisse: "Are you happy?" (Bradbury, Part One). This question triggers Montag's realization of the emptiness of his existence under a censored regime and sparks his quest for truth and understanding.

Let's look further into this theme, examining its multifaceted representation in the novel.

1. **Censorship as a Means of Control**:

   ○ **Government's Role**: The government in "Fahrenheit 451" exercises its power by censoring literature and controlling information. Beatty explains to Montag, "If you don't want a man unhappy politically, don't give him two sides to a question to worry him; give him one. Better yet, give him none" (Bradbury, Part One). This philosophy underlines the government's strategy to maintain order by eliminating the complexities and ambiguities that accompany diverse viewpoints.

   ○ **Firemen as Censors**: Firemen, like Montag, are the instruments of this censorship. Initially, Montag does not question his role, illustrating how the oppressive system co-opts individuals into perpetuating its agenda. His unquestioning compliance represents society's willingness to accept censorship for perceived stability and happiness.

2. **Impact of Censorship on Society**:

   ○ **Loss of Depth and Meaning**: The novel portrays a society obsessed with superficial entertainment, like Mildred's immersion in the interactive television 'parlor walls.' This obsession reflects the broader societal malaise stemming from the absence of meaningful, thought-provoking content, a direct result of censorship. The superficiality of Montag's society highlights the intellectual and emotional void created by the absence of literature and free thought.

   ○ **Degradation of Human Relationships**: The lack of depth

in human relationships is another casualty of this censorship. Montag's relationship with his wife, Mildred, is characterized by emotional disconnect and lack of genuine communication, symbolizing the broader societal decay.

3. Censorship's Role in Suppressing Dissent:

○ **Intellectual Conformity**: Beatty's dialogues often reflect the government's desire to create a homogeneous society. He articulates, "We must all be alike. Not everyone born free and equal, as the Constitution says, but everyone made equal" (Bradbury, Part One). This pursuit of sameness through censorship is shown as a way to suppress dissent and prevent any form of uprising or challenge to the status quo.

○ **Fear of Ideas**: The society in "Fahrenheit 451" fears ideas that books represent. This fear is not just of dissent but also of the transformative power of knowledge and thought. It is a fear of the introspection and self-awareness that books can provoke, elements that are essential for individual growth but potentially destabilizing for a conformist society.

4. Montag's Transformation as a Challenge to Censorship:

○ **Awakening to Censorship's Harm**: Montag's journey from a compliant fireman to a rebellious seeker of knowledge embodies the human spirit's resistance to intellectual oppression. His growing disillusionment with his society's values and his eventual rebellion symbolize the potential for individual awakening and challenge to oppressive regimes.

○ **Pursuit of Knowledge**: Montag's thirst for knowledge, ignited by his interactions with Clarisse and fueled by his secret hoarding of books, becomes a personal rebellion against the intellectual oppression he has been part of. His transformation is a beacon of hope in the narrative, suggesting that the human desire for understanding and truth can prevail even in the most oppressive circumstances.

In conclusion, the theme of censorship and intellectual oppression in "Fahrenheit 451" serves as a stark warning against the dangers of suppressing free thought and expression. Bradbury masterfully illustrates how such a regime can lead to a hollow, disconnected society, devoid of the depth and richness that literature and free intellectual inquiry bring. Montag's journey highlights the enduring value of dissent and the irreplaceable role of literature and knowledge in fostering a vibrant, thoughtful society.

DESTRUCTIVE IMPACT OF TECHNOLOGY

"The Destructive Impact of Technology" is a prevalent theme in "Fahrenheit 451," offering a critical examination of how technological advancements, while ostensibly beneficial, can lead to societal degradation when misused or overemphasized. Bradbury's portrayal of a future where technology dominates and diminishes human experience serves as a cautionary tale about the potential pitfalls of unbridled technological reliance. Let us explore this theme in detail, drawing upon specific references from the novel to substantiate our analysis.

1. **Technology as a Tool for Distraction and Control**:

   ○ **The 'Parlor Walls'**: A quintessential example of technology's destructive impact is seen in the 'parlor walls,' large, immersive television screens that dominate people's homes. Mildred, Montag's wife, is addicted to these screens, which provide a constant stream of mindless entertainment. She refers to the characters on the screens as her 'family,' illustrating her deep disconnection from reality: "My 'family' is people. They tell me things; I laugh, they laugh! And the colors!" (Bradbury, Part One). This illustrates how technology can be used to manipulate reality, creating an artificial sense of connection while simultaneously isolating individuals from genuine human interaction.

2. **Suppression of Intellectual Growth**:

○ **The Seashell Radios**: Another technological device, the 'seashell' earbuds, are used by characters like Mildred to remain constantly tuned into entertainment or government propaganda, effectively drowning out their own thoughts and the real world around them. These devices symbolize how technology can suppress intellectual curiosity and critical thinking, keeping the populace in a state of passive consumption and complacency.

3. **Technology and Dehumanization**:

○ **The Mechanical Hound**: The Mechanical Hound, a robotic enforcer used by the firemen, represents the more sinister aspects of technology. Programmed to hunt down and kill those who defy societal norms (e.g., by reading books), the Hound embodies the dehumanizing effect of technology when it is wielded as a tool of oppression. Its lack of empathy and mechanical precision in executing its tasks illustrate a society where technology has superseded human values and ethical considerations.

4. **Contrast with Nature and Human Connection**:

○ **Clarisse's Perspective**: Clarisse McClellan serves as a foil to the technology-obsessed society. She enjoys walking in the rain, observing the natural world, and engaging in meaningful conversations — activities that are deemed odd in Montag's society. Her interactions with Montag highlight the stark contrast between a life enriched by human connection and nature, and one dulled by technological distractions.

5. **Consequences for Society**:

- ○ **Societal Apathy and Decay**: The novel depicts a society that has become apathetic and emotionally stunted, largely due to its overreliance on technology. The lack of meaningful relationships, the absence of critical discourse, and the suppression of dissenting ideas have led to a superficial and disconnected society. The widespread acceptance of this technology-driven lifestyle illustrates the broader societal decay, a consequence of prioritizing technological advancement over humanistic values.

In conclusion, the theme of "The Destructive Impact of Technology" in "Fahrenheit 451" serves as a powerful warning about the potential dangers of technology when it supersedes human interaction and intellectual growth. Bradbury's depiction of a society enthralled by technology, yet devoid of genuine human connection and critical thought, underscores the need for balance between technological advancements and the preservation of humanistic values. The novel invites readers to reflect on their own relationship with technology, emphasizing the importance of maintaining a connection with the natural world and fostering meaningful human relationships.

Knowledge and Human Understanding

The theme of Knowledge and Human Understanding in "Fahrenheit 451" is a fundamental thread that weaves through the narrative, underscoring the importance of intellectual freedom and the pursuit of knowledge to achieve true understanding and enlightenment. This theme is manifested in various aspects of the novel, from the protagonist's journey to the societal dynamics at play. Let's delve into an in-depth analysis of how Bradbury explores this theme, highlighting key references and moments from the novel.

1. **Value of Books and Knowledge**:

   ○ **Books as Vessels of Knowledge**: In Bradbury's dystopian society, books are banned because they are considered sources of discord and confusion. However, the novel portrays books as essential repositories of knowledge and wisdom. Professor Faber, a key character who aids Montag in his quest for understanding, eloquently encapsulates this when he says to Montag, "The magic is only in what books say, how they stitched the patches of the universe together into one garment for us" (Bradbury, Part Two). This metaphor highlights the transformative power of books to expand human understanding, offering insights into life and the world.

   ○ **Books as Reflections of Humanity**: The novel suggests that books are not merely collections of words, but reflections of human thoughts, experiences, and emotions. They are shown as tools for preserving human history, culture, and diversity of thought, essential for a holistic understanding of the human condition.

2. **Quest for Personal Enlightenment**:

- ○ **Montag's Transformation**: The protagonist, Guy Montag, begins as a fireman who burns books without questioning his role. His encounter with Clarisse McClellan, a young woman who questions the status quo, ignites Montag's journey towards enlightenment. His growing dissatisfaction with his empty life leads him to seek knowledge and understanding through the forbidden act of reading. Montag's transformation is a testament to the human desire for deeper understanding and the power of knowledge to change one's perspective.

- ○ **Clarisse as a Catalyst**: Clarisse's role in the novel is pivotal in sparking Montag's quest for knowledge. Her curiosity, appreciation for nature, and penchant for reflective thinking contrast starkly with the prevailing societal norms. She represents an uncorrupted view of the world, one that values understanding over ignorance.

3. **Knowledge vs. Ignorance**:

- ○ **Society's Fear of Intellectualism**: The novel portrays a society that fears intellectualism and critical thinking. Captain Beatty, the antagonist, represents this fear when he explains the rationale behind book burning, emphasizing how books can lead to discontent and unhappiness (Bradbury, Part One). This reflects the theme that ignorance is often used as a tool for control and that knowledge is seen as a threat to conformity and uniformity.

○ **Consequences of Intellectual Apathy**: The society in "Fahrenheit 451" is characterized by a lack of intellectual depth and meaningful discourse, leading to a shallow, unfulfilling existence. The rampant consumerism and mindless entertainment that dominate the lives of citizens serve as a distraction from critical thought and self-reflection.

4. **The Role of Knowledge in Human Connection**:

○ **Fostering Empathy and Understanding**: The novel suggests that knowledge and understanding are key to fostering empathy and genuine human connection. Montag's exposure to literature enlightens him intellectually and awakens his emotional capacities, enabling him to connect with others on a deeper level.

○ **The 'Book People' as Preservers of Knowledge**: The novel concludes with Montag joining a group of individuals who have memorized books to preserve their content. This act symbolizes the enduring nature of knowledge and its ability to connect people across time and space.

This theme is not just a backdrop but central to the novel's critique of a dystopian society where intellectual curiosity is suppressed in favor of conformist ideals. So, let's further explore this theme, examining its nuances and implications throughout the novel.

1. **Knowledge as a Path to Freedom**:

○ **Montag's Enlightenment**: Guy Montag's transformation from a compliant fireman to a seeker of knowledge is a

poignant representation of this theme. His initial contentment with his life is shattered when he begins to question the
purpose and ethics of his job: "He was not happy. He was not
happy. He said the words to himself. He recognized this as
the true state of affairs" (Bradbury, Part One). This realization
propels him on a journey towards enlightenment, symbolizing the power of knowledge to liberate individuals from the
shackles of ignorance and conformity.

- **Faber's Philosophy**: Professor Faber, a mentor figure to
  Montag, articulates the value of books and knowledge, stating, "The magic is only in what books say, how they stitched
  the patches of the universe together into one garment for us"
  (Bradbury, Part Two). Faber's words underscore the idea that
  knowledge is not just about acquiring information; it's about
  understanding the interconnectedness of ideas and experiences, which leads to a deeper comprehension of the world and
  oneself.

2. Contrast Between Knowledge and Ignorance:

- **Societal Apathy**: The stark contrast between knowledge and
  ignorance is highlighted by depicting Montag's society. The
  populace is engrossed in shallow entertainment, rendering
  them oblivious to the deeper truths of their existence. This societal apathy directly results from the government's censorship
  and the discouragement of intellectual pursuits, illustrating
  how the lack of knowledge can lead to a hollow, unfulfilled
  existence.

- **Beatty's Manipulation of Knowledge**: Captain Beatty, the
  antagonist, represents a perverse manipulation of knowledge.

He is well-read and uses his understanding of literature to justify the government's policies and to manipulate Montag. Beatty's character demonstrates that knowledge, in the hands of those seeking to control and oppress, can be twisted to serve harmful ends.

3. **Rediscovery of Lost Knowledge**:

- **Montag's Rebellion**: Montag's decision to read and understand the books he was meant to burn is an act of rebellion against societal norms. His growing disillusionment with society and his quest for truth represent a rediscovery of lost knowledge, a theme that speaks to the resilience of the human spirit in the face of oppressive forces.

- **The 'Book People'**: The novel culminates with Montag joining a group of individuals who memorize books to preserve their content. This act of rebellion against intellectual oppression symbolizes the enduring nature of knowledge and its role in human survival and progress.

4. **Knowledge and Empathy**:

- **Understanding and Connection**: The theme also touches on the idea that knowledge leads to empathy and human connection. Through his journey, Montag develops a deeper understanding of himself and others, showcasing how knowledge fosters empathy, an essential component of meaningful human relationships.

- **Clarisse's Influence**: Clarisse McClellan's role in the novel is crucial in this aspect. Her questioning nature and appreciation for the world around her offer a stark contrast to the prevailing societal norms and inspire Montag to seek knowledge and understanding.

In conclusion, the theme of Knowledge and Human Understanding in "Fahrenheit 451" is a profound commentary on the importance of intellectual freedom and the pursuit of truth. Bradbury masterfully illustrates how knowledge can be a force for personal liberation and societal change, while also warning of the dangers when it is suppressed or manipulated. The novel ultimately champions the transformative power of learning and the vital role that intellectual curiosity plays in shaping a just and enlightened society.

Conformity vs. Individuality

The theme of Conformity vs. Individuality in "Fahrenheit 451" is a critical exploration of the tension between societal pressure to conform and the individual's desire for self-expression and independent thought. This theme is a vital undercurrent that flows through the narrative, highlighting the struggle of characters as they navigate a world that demands uniformity at the expense of personal freedom. Let's examine this theme in detail, referencing specific moments from the novel.

1. **Societal Pressure for Conformity**:

   ○ **Homogeneity as a Social Ideal**: The society in "Fahrenheit 451" is predicated on the idea that happiness and social stability are achieved through uniformity of thought and action. Captain Beatty, representing the government's ideology, articulates this when he tells Montag, "We must all be alike. Not everyone born free and equal, as the Constitution says, but everyone made equal" (Bradbury, Part One). This statement reflects the overarching societal goal of eliminating differences to prevent conflict and ensure a superficial sense of harmony.

   ○ **Role of Firemen in Enforcing Conformity**: The firemen in the novel are the enforcers of conformity, tasked with destroying books, which are seen as sources of discordant ideas. The burning of books is symbolic of the eradication of individual thought, as Montag reflects in the beginning, enjoying the flames: "It was a pleasure to burn. It was a special pleasure to see things eaten, to see things blackened and changed" (Bradbury, Part One).

2. **Struggle for Individuality**:

- **Montag's Transformation**: Montag's journey from a conformist fireman to a rebellious seeker of knowledge epitomizes the struggle for individuality. His meeting with Clarisse McClellan, who asks, "Are you happy?" (Bradbury, Part One), ignites his quest for individual understanding, challenging the status quo of his society.

- **Clarisse as an Emblem of Individuality**: Clarisse represents the embodiment of individuality in the novel. Her curiosity, love for nature, and penchant for reflective thinking contrast sharply with the prevailing societal norms. She is described as "odd" because of her unique perspective, illustrating how individuality is viewed as an anomaly in this conformist society.

3. **Consequences of Conformity**:

- **Loss of Depth in Human Experience**: The novel portrays a hollow and emotionally barren society, a direct result of its insistence on conformity. Mildred, Montag's wife, is an example of a life lived in compliance with societal norms. Her addiction to the 'parlor walls' and disconnection from reality highlight the emptiness of a life devoid of individual thought.

- **Deterioration of Human Relationships**: The lack of individuality also impacts human relationships, as seen in the estrangement between Montag and Mildred. Their marriage lacks genuine communication and emotional depth, emblematic of a society that values conformity over personal connections.

4. **Individuality as a Means of Resistance**:

- **Montag's Rebellion**: Montag's eventual rebellion, his decision to read and understand the books he is meant to burn, is a powerful act of reclaiming his individuality. His transformation signifies the potential for individual resistance against oppressive societal norms.

- **The 'Book People'**: The group of individuals who memorize books at the end of the novel symbolizes the preservation of individual thought against societal conformity. They represent the hope that individuality, preserved through knowledge, can survive and possibly revive a more open and free society.

Expanding further on the theme, we find that this theme not only critiques societal norms but also delves into the psychological and moral dimensions of its characters. It becomes a narrative thread that intertwines personal identity with broader societal structures, revealing a complex web of influences and consequences. Let's explore this theme in greater depth:

1. **Conformity as Socially Engineered Comfort**:

- Comfort vs. Truth: The society in "Fahrenheit 451" has been structured to prioritize comfort over truth and convenience over challenge. Beatty's lecture to Montag highlights this, as he explains the rationale behind the ban on books: society chose to abandon books in favor of simpler, more digestible forms of entertainment. This societal choice represents a deliberate move towards conformity to avoid the discomfort that often accompanies individual thought and critical analysis.

○ **Reference**: "Don't give them any slippery stuff like philosophy or sociology to tie things up with. That way lies melancholy" (Bradbury, Part One).

2. Individuality as a Threat to Order:

○ **Perceived Danger of Diversity**: In Bradbury's envisioned society, individuality – especially in the form of diverse ideas and critical thinking – is viewed as a threat to the homogeneity and order of the community. This is exemplified in the character of Clarisse, whose mere presence and unconventional views pose a challenge to Montag's previously unexamined life.

○ **Reference**: Clarisse's uncle describes the past society: "They all sounded like the others" (Bradbury, Part One), highlighting the loss of individuality in pursuit of uniformity.

3. Montag's Internal Conflict:

○ **Struggle Between Conformity and Desire for Knowledge**: Montag's character arc is a powerful exploration of the internal conflict between societal conformity and the desire for knowledge and individual understanding. His initial satisfaction with his life gives way to a profound sense of unease, eventually leading him to question and reject the society's norms.

○ **Reference**: Montag's reflection on his life and job: "He wore his happiness like a mask and the girl had run off across the lawn with the mask and there was no way of going to knock on her door and ask for it back" (Bradbury, Part One).

4. **Resistance Through Preservation of Knowledge**:

- ◦ **The 'Book People' as Symbols of Resistance**: The 'Book People,' Montag encounters at the end of the novel, embody resistance to conformity. Each person memorizes a book to ensure the preservation of diverse ideas and knowledge, symbolizing the triumph of individual thought over societal suppression.

- ◦ **Reference**: Granger, the leader of the 'Book People,' describes their mission: "We're remembering" (Bradbury, Part Three).

5. **Transformation as a Vehicle for Individuality**:

- ◦ **Montag's Journey as a Metaphor**: Montag's transformation from a conforming fireman to an individual seeking enlightenment symbolizes the broader theme of individuality. His journey underscores the idea that true fulfillment and understanding come from embracing one's individual thoughts and questioning the world, rather than accepting a preordained role.

- ◦ **Reference**: Montag's realization: "I don't know anything any more" (Bradbury, Part Three), signifies his break from conformity and the beginning of his individual journey.

In conclusion, the theme of Conformity vs. Individuality in "Fahrenheit 451" is a profound exploration of the human condition, questioning the value of societal norms that demand conformity at the expense of personal growth and understanding. Bradbury's narrative skillfully illustrates the tension between these two forces, ultimately advocating for the importance of individual thought, the pursuit of knowledge, and the courage to challenge the status quo. The novel remains a timeless reminder of the significance of maintaining one's identity and beliefs in the face of societal pressure.

Transformation and Redemption

The theme of Transformation and Redemption in "Fahrenheit 451" is a poignant element that underscores the capacity for personal growth and moral awakening in the face of oppressive societal norms. This theme is vividly illustrated through the character arc of Guy Montag, the protagonist, as well as through the broader narrative of a society in flux. Let's explore this theme, highlighting how Bradbury weaves this critical motif into the fabric of his novel.

1. **Montag's Personal Transformation**:

   - **Initial Complacency**: Montag begins the novel as a typical fireman, complacent in his role of burning books and suppressing intellectual freedom. His transformation begins with his interactions with Clarisse McClellan, who introduces him to a world of beauty and questioning. Montag's initial satisfaction with his life is depicted early on, when he is described as enjoying his work: "It was a pleasure to burn. It was a special pleasure to see things eaten, to see things blackened and changed" (Bradbury, Part One).

   - **Awakening to Awareness**: Clarisse's questions and Montag's subsequent discovery of his wife Mildred's attempted suicide serve as catalysts for his transformation. He begins to question the society's values and his role in it, leading to an internal conflict and a growing sense of disillusionment with his life and work.

2. **Quest for Knowledge and Understanding**:

- **Rebellion Against Societal Norms**: Montag's transformation is marked by his rebellion against the societal norms of censorship and conformity. He secretly begins to read books, seeking knowledge and understanding that has been forbidden. This act of rebellion is a significant step in his journey toward redemption.

- **Reference**: Montag's realization of his need for change is evident when he thinks, "There must be something in books, things we can't imagine, to make a woman stay in a burning house; there must be something there. You don't stay for nothing" (Bradbury, Part One).

3. **Mentorship and Guidance**:

- **Faber's Influence**: Professor Faber plays a crucial role in Montag's transformation. He acts as a mentor, providing guidance and support as Montag navigates his newfound quest for knowledge. Faber helps Montag understand the importance of literature and the role it plays in human understanding and empathy.

- **Reference**: Faber explains to Montag, "The magic is only in what books say, how they stitched the patches of the universe together into one garment for us" (Bradbury, Part Two).

4. **Montag's Act of Redemption**:

- **Breaking Free**: Montag's transformation culminates in his decision to break free from his past life and seek a new path. This is symbolized by his dramatic act of killing Captain Beatty, a figure representing the oppressive societal order, and his escape from the city.

○ **Reference**: During his escape, Montag reflects on his actions and newfound purpose: "And as before, he was surprised to find himself feeling no guilt at all" (Bradbury, Part Three).

5. Hope for Renewal:

○ **Joining the 'Book People'**: The final stages of Montag's transformation and redemption are seen in his joining the 'Book People,' a group dedicated to preserving knowledge through memorizing books. This act symbolizes not only Montag's personal redemption but also a hope for the renewal of society.

○ **Reference**: Granger, the leader of the 'Book People,' welcomes Montag, symbolizing the acceptance of his transformation: "Welcome back from the dead" (Bradbury, Part Three).

The theme is central to Guy Montag's character development and serves as a broader allegorical narrative about societal change and the potential for collective redemption. This theme encapsulates the journey from ignorance to awareness, apathy to empathy, and oppression to liberation. Let's explore its various facets and implications throughout the novel.

1. Montag's Evolving Self-Perception:

○ **From Fireman to Rebel**: Montag's transformation is a metamorphosis from a fireman who blindly follows orders to burn books to a rebel who seeks to understand and preserve them. Initially proud of his role, as indicated by the description of his fiery work in the opening pages, Montag gradually becomes disillusioned with the hollow values of his society. This shift is marked by his growing discomfort with his actions and the system he represents.

- **Reference**: Montag's internal conflict is evident in his reflections: "He felt his body divide itself into a hotness and a coldness, a softness and a hardness, a trembling and a not trembling, the two halves grinding one upon the other" (Bradbury, Part Two).

2. **Influence of Key Characters on Montag's Transformation**:

- **Clarisse's Role**: Clarisse McClellan is a catalyst for Montag's transformation. Her inquisitive nature and appreciation for the world's beauty challenge Montag's perceptions and ignite his quest for knowledge. Clarisse's questioning of whether Montag is happy serves as the initial spark for his journey of self-discovery.

- **Faber's Guidance**: Faber, a retired English professor, plays a crucial role in deepening Montag's understanding of literature and its significance. He provides intellectual and moral support, helping Montag navigate his newfound awareness and the complexities of their society.

- **Reference**: Faber's influence is significant when he communicates through the earpiece, guiding Montag during critical moments, such as Montag's confrontation with Beatty.

3. **Redemption through Knowledge and Resistance**:

- **Montag's Quest for Literacy**: Montag's transformation is marked by his illicit pursuit of literacy. The act of reading and understanding becomes a form of resistance and redemption for him. Through this process, Montag gains knowledge and develops a moral conscience and empathy.

- **Reference**: Montag's reading of books, despite the risk, as when he reads poetry to Mildred and her friends, represents his defiance of societal norms and his journey towards redemption.

4. **Symbolism of Fire**:

- **Fire as Destruction and Enlightenment**: Initially, fire represents destruction and oppression in Montag's role as a fireman. However, as Montag transforms, fire takes on a new meaning – it becomes a symbol of enlightenment and renewal. This dual symbolism of fire reflects Montag's journey from a destructive agent to a bearer of light and knowledge.

- **Reference**: Montag's change in perception of fire is symbolized in his final interaction with fire, as he joins the 'Book People' and sees the fire as warmth and comfort rather than a tool for destruction (Bradbury, Part Three).

5. **Transformation as a Path to Societal Redemption**:

- **Beyond Individual Change**: Montag's personal transformation also symbolizes the potential for societal redemption. Through the 'Book People,' the novel suggests that redemption and renewal are possible on a larger scale, even in a society steeped in censorship and oppression.

- **Reference**: The novel's ending, with Montag joining the

'Book People' and witnessing the city's destruction, signifies a hope for rebirth and a new beginning based on knowledge and understanding.

In conclusion, the theme of Transformation and Redemption in "Fahrenheit 451" is a multi-layered exploration of personal and societal change. Bradbury skillfully illustrates how individual awakening can lead to a broader societal transformation. Montag's journey from ignorance to enlightenment, from conformity to resistance, encapsulates the novel's message of hope and the enduring power of the human spirit to seek truth and redemption. This theme is a testament to the transformative power of knowledge and the resilience of individuals in the face of oppressive societal norms.

The Role of Art and Culture in Society

The theme of The Role of Art and Culture in Society in "Fahrenheit 451" is intricately interwoven into the narrative, offering a profound commentary on how art and culture shape human experience and societal values. In Bradbury's dystopian world, where books are banned, and intellectualism is shunned, the absence of art and culture leads to a society devoid of depth and meaning. Let's explore this theme further, drawing upon specific references from the novel.

1. **Art and Culture as Sources of Reflection and Challenge**:

   ○ **Censorship of Books**: The government's censorship of books directly attacks art and culture. Books are seen as dangerous because they provoke thought, reflection, and potentially challenge the status quo. Captain Beatty explains this to Montag: "Books were only one type of receptacle where we stored a lot of things we were afraid we might forget" (Bradbury, Part One). This statement underscores the perceived threat of art and culture in their ability to evoke questioning and introspection.

   ○ **Suppression of Individuality**: The suppression of books, which represent the pinnacle of art and culture, is also a suppression of individual thought and creativity. This enforced uniformity leads to a society lacking in diversity of ideas and perspectives.

2. Art as a Means of Emotional and Intellectual Engagement:

- **Montag's Awakening**: Montag's interaction with books and his subsequent emotional and intellectual awakening highlight the role of art and culture in stimulating human consciousness. When Montag reads Dover Beach to Mildred and her friends, he is moved by the beauty and depth of the poem, which starkly contrasts with the superficial entertainment of his society.

- **Reference**: The poem evokes a response from Mrs. Phelps, one of Mildred's friends, who is moved to tears, indicating the power of art to evoke emotional depth: "How long is it since you were really bothered? About something important, about something real?" (Bradbury, Part Two).

3. Culture as a Reflection of Humanity:

- **Cultural Memory and Identity**: The 'Book People' at the end of the novel represents the preservation of cultural memory and identity. Each person memorizes a book, ensuring that the essence of culture and art survives even in a society that seeks to obliterate it.

- **Reference**: Granger, the leader of the 'Book People,' explains their purpose: "We're not important. We're not anything. The important thing is the knowledge, the information" (Bradbury, Part Three). This highlights the idea that art and culture are vital to maintaining a sense of history and identity.

4. Contrast Between a Cultured and an Uncultured Society:

- **Societal Decay**: The novel depicts a society in decay, primarily due to the absence of art and culture. The contrast between this decay and the rich intellectual life represented by books underscores the role of art and culture in nurturing a healthy, vibrant society.

○ **Mechanical Hound as a Symbol**: The Mechanical Hound, a tool for suppressing dissent and intellectualism, symbolizes the absence of culture and the dominance of a sterile, technological society over a cultured, humanistic one.

It's evident that this theme is not merely a background element but a critical lens through which the narrative explores the complex relationship between society, knowledge, and human expression. This theme is multifaceted, touching upon the preservation of history, the nurturing of critical thought, and the expression of human emotion and experience. Let's travel deeper into this theme:

1. **Art and Culture as Tools for Critical Thought and Resistance**:

   ○ **Intellectual Resistance**: In "Fahrenheit 451," books symbolize not just knowledge, but also a form of resistance against a society that seeks to suppress individual thought. The act of reading and engaging with literature is depicted as a rebellious act, a means of preserving independent thinking in an oppressive regime.

   ○ **Reference**: This is exemplified when Montag reads and finds solace in books, a direct defiance of societal norms: "He opened to read: 'It was a pleasure to burn'" (Bradbury, Part Two). The irony of Montag reading this line, which opens the novel, underscores his transformation and resistance.

2. Cultural Amnesia and Societal Decline:

○ **Loss of Historical Context**: The novel portrays a society that has lost its historical and cultural context due to the suppression of books. This loss results in a populace that lacks understanding of their past, diminishing their ability to assess the present and envision a different future critically.

○ **Reference**: Captain Beatty's speeches to Montag often touch on historical context, yet they are used to justify the current state of society, revealing a twisted interpretation of history: "Classics cut to fifteen-minute radio shows" (Bradbury, Part One).

3. Art as an Expression of Human Experience:

○ **Emotional Depth and Empathy**: Literature and art are shown as mediums that convey the depth and complexity of human emotions and experiences. They provide a window into the lives and feelings of others, fostering empathy and understanding, which are conspicuously absent in the novel's society.

○ **Reference**: The emotional reaction elicited when Montag reads poetry to Mildred and her friends demonstrates the power of literature to touch the human soul: "And the women sat there, frozen" (Bradbury, Part Two).

4. Art and Culture as Foundations of Identity:

○ **Individual and Collective Identity**: Through its characters, the novel suggests that art and culture are integral to both individual and collective identity. The 'Book People' at the end of the novel memorize books to ensure the survival of cultural and intellectual diversity, preserving individual and societal identities.

- ◦ **Reference**: When Granger explains their mission, "We're remembering," (Bradbury, Part Three), it underscores the role of art and culture in shaping and maintaining identity.

5. **Contrast Between a Cultured and a Sterile Society**:

- ◦ **Mechanization vs. Humanism**: The stark contrast between the mechanized, sterile society and the rich, humanistic world represented by books highlights the importance of art and culture in humanizing individuals and society. The Mechanical Hound, as a symbol of technological control, contrasts with the human warmth and depth found in literature.

- ◦ **Reference**: The description of the Mechanical Hound, "It was like a great bee come home from the field" (Bradbury, Part One), contrasts with the human warmth evoked in the poetic passages Montag reads.

In conclusion, the theme of The Role of Art and Culture in Society in "Fahrenheit 451" is a profound exploration of how art and culture are essential to the human experience. Bradbury's narrative vividly illustrates the impoverishment of a society devoid of these elements, showcasing the necessity of art and culture in fostering critical thinking, emotional depth, and a sense of identity and continuity. The novel is a testament to the enduring power of literature and culture in challenging oppressive norms and enriching the human spirit.

Rebirth and Hope

The theme of Rebirth and Hope in Ray Bradbury's "Fahrenheit 451" is a powerful motif that emerges especially towards the latter part of the narrative, offering a sense of optimism and the possibility of a new beginning in the aftermath of destruction and despair. This theme is intricately tied to the novel's overall message about the resilience of the human spirit and the enduring value of knowledge. Let's explore how Bradbury weaves this theme into his work, with references to the text for a comprehensive understanding.

The Phoenix Symbolism:

1. **Symbol of Renewal**: The Phoenix, a mythical bird that is reborn from its ashes, is a recurring symbol in the novel, representing the cyclical nature of destruction and rebirth. Captain Beatty refers to this symbol when he talks to Montag, saying, "Every fireman, sooner or later, hits this. They only need understanding, to know how the wheels run. Need to know the history of our profession. They don't feed it to rookies like they used to. Damn shame" followed by a reference to the Phoenix (Bradbury, Part One). This reference to the Phoenix sets the stage for the novel's overarching theme of rebirth and hope.

2. **Montag's Transformation**: Montag's personal journey can also be seen as a Phoenix-like rebirth. From the ashes of his former life as a fireman, he emerges as a new person, committed to preserving

knowledge and seeking a deeper understanding of the world.

Destruction of the City:

1. **Catastrophic Yet Cleansing**: The destruction of the city in the novel's climax serves as both a catastrophic end and a potential beginning. The obliteration of the city, caused by a war that has been looming in the background, can be seen as a form of societal rebirth, a chance to start anew.

2. **Reference**: As Montag and the 'Book People' witness the destruction, Bradbury describes it as a distant, yet impactful event: "The city was gone" (Bradbury, Part Three). This dramatic moment underscores the theme of rebirth and hope amidst devastation.

The 'Book People' as Harbingers of Hope:

1. **Preservation of Knowledge**: The group of individuals Montag encounters, known as the 'Book People,' symbolize hope for the future. Each person has memorized a book, ensuring that, even in the face of widespread censorship and destruction, knowledge and culture are preserved.

2. **Reference**: Granger, the leader of the 'Book People,' shares his vision with Montag: "We're remembering" (Bradbury, Part Three). This act of remembering and preserving knowledge is a beacon of hope, suggesting that rebirth and renewal are possible through the continuity of human thought and culture.

Montag's Role in a Hopeful Future:

1. **A New Purpose**: Montag's integration into the 'Book People' marks his own rebirth and signifies his role in the hopeful rebuilding of society. He is no longer the destroyer of knowledge but a

guardian of it.

2. **Reference**: Montag's realization of his new role is evident when he remembers a passage from the Bible: "To everything there is a season. A time to break down, and a time to build up" (Bradbury, Part Three). This reference encapsulates the theme of rebirth and the hope that comes with new beginnings.

It becomes increasingly clear that this theme is pivotal in offering a resolution to the novel's narrative arc and its philosophical and moral quandaries. The theme serves as a beacon of optimism, suggesting that despite the darkest times, there is always a potential for renewal and positive change. Let's examine this theme further, considering its various dimensions and implications within the context of the novel.

Hope Amidst Desolation:

1. **The Aftermath of Destruction**: The destruction of the city in the novel's climax is both literal and symbolic. While it signifies the end of a society steeped in censorship and superficiality, it also represents a clean slate. The annihilation paves the way for the possibility of a new society built on more enlightened principles.

2. **Reference**: As Montag and the 'Book People' view the destruction from afar, Bradbury describes, "The city was gone" (Bradbury, Part Three). This powerful imagery sets the stage for the theme of rebirth, suggesting a new beginning emerging from the ashes of the old.

The Role of Memory and Preservation:

1. **Cultural Continuity**: The 'Book People' are not just survivors but are the carriers of hope for the future. Their commitment to memorizing books ensures the survival of human knowledge and

culture, even in the face of total societal collapse.

2. **Reference**: Granger's comparison of humans to a Phoenix that can learn from its mistakes: "And when we remember that, and cease making the same damn insane mistakes!" (Bradbury, Part Three), highlights the hope for human society to rebuild itself more wisely.

Montag's Personal Rebirth:

1. **From Conformity to Enlightenment**: Montag's transformation symbolizes a personal rebirth. He transitions from a passive participant in a repressive society to an active seeker of truth and preservationist of knowledge. His journey is a microcosm of the larger societal transformation that Bradbury envisions.

2. **Reference**: Montag's reflection on his past and future signifies this transformation: "He was not empty. There was more than enough here to fill him" (Bradbury, Part Three). This marks Montag's character embodying hope and renewal.

Hope as a Driver of Change:

1. **Potential for a New Society**: The novel concludes with the prospect of a new society that learns from past mistakes. This hopeful vision is encapsulated in the group of individuals dedicated to preserving knowledge, suggesting that change is possible even in the bleakest of circumstances.

2. **Reference**: The final lines of the novel, where Montag recalls the Biblical verse of Ecclesiastes, "To everything there is a season. A time to break down, and a time to build up" (Bradbury, Part Three), encapsulates the cyclical nature of destruction and

rebirth, and the perpetual hope for a better future.

In conclusion, the theme of Rebirth and Hope in "Fahrenheit 451" is a powerful testament to the resilience of the human spirit and the enduring power of knowledge and culture. Bradbury masterfully weaves this theme into the narrative, providing a counterpoint to the dystopian aspects of the novel and offering a vision of redemption and renewal. The theme resonates with a message of optimism, suggesting that even in the face of overwhelming adversity, there is always the possibility for growth, change, and a brighter future. This theme not only concludes the novel on a hopeful note but also invites readers to reflect on the potential for transformation in their own lives and societies.

Main Characters

"Fahrenheit 451" by Ray Bradbury features a cast of characters, each embodying different facets of the dystopian society in which they live. Their interactions and transformations are central to the novel's exploration of themes such as censorship, the role of technology, and the quest for knowledge. Here's a detailed look at the main characters:

1. **Guy Montag**:

   ○ **Role**: Montag is the protagonist of the novel, a fireman whose job is to burn books.

   ○ **Characterization**:

      • Initially, Montag was a dutiful citizen who took pride in his work.

      • He undergoes a significant transformation sparked by his interactions with Clarisse McClellan and his growing disillusionment with society.

      • Montag evolves into a reflective and rebellious character, seeking knowledge and questioning societal norms.

   ○ **Significance**: Montag's journey from conformity to rebellion represents the human capacity for change and the importance of individual thought.

2. **Clarisse McClellan**:

  ○ **Role**: A young woman who becomes Montag's neighbor and friend.

  ○ **Characterization**:

    • Clarisse is depicted as curious, thoughtful, and inquisitive, contrasting sharply with the conformist society around her.

    • She enjoys nature, deep conversations, and questions everything, embodying a sense of wonder and skepticism about the world.

  ○ **Significance**: Clarisse acts as a catalyst for Montag's transformation, representing the power of questioning and critical thinking in a complacent society.

3. **Mildred Montag**:

  ○ **Role**: Montag's wife.

  ○ **Characterization**:

    • Mildred is deeply immersed in the shallow culture of their society, constantly engaged with the interactive television screens and radio.

    • She is emotionally detached and indifferent to Montag's internal turmoil and the larger problems of their society.

  ○ **Significance**: Mildred represents the apathetic and disconnected populace, illustrating the numbing effects of technology and the consequences of a life devoid of real human connection or intellectual curiosity.

4. Captain Beatty:

- **Role**: The fire chief and Montag's boss.

- **Characterization**:

  - Beatty is articulate, intelligent, and understands the implications of books and ideas. However, he staunchly defends the book-burning policy and the reasons for societal censorship.

  - He presents as both a mentor and antagonist to Montag, offering insights into their world while also seeking to maintain control over Montag.

- **Significance**: Beatty represents the complexities of the dystopian society, embodying the contradictions and the dark side of intellectualism when it is used to justify oppression.

5. Professor Faber:

- **Role**: A retired English professor who assists Montag.

- **Characterization**:

  - Faber is a cautious but wise man, who understands the value of literature and critical thought.

  - He provides Montag with guidance and support as he navigates his newfound awareness and plans to challenge the status quo.

○ **Significance**: Faber symbolizes the remnants of intellectualism and knowledge in a society that has largely abandoned these values. He plays a crucial role in Montag's transformation and the broader theme of preserving knowledge against oppressive forces.

These characters collectively illustrate the varied responses of individuals to a society that enforces conformity, suppresses intellectual freedom, and discourages individual thought. Through them, Bradbury paints a vivid picture of the struggles and triumphs that come with seeking truth in a world that often seeks to hide it.

Describe Guy Montag

Guy Montag, the central character in "Fahrenheit 451," is a complex figure whose development drives the narrative and embodies the novel's key themes. His journey from a conformist fireman to a questioning rebel provides profound insights into the human condition under a repressive regime. Let's look into Montag's character in a detailed manner:

1. **Montag's Initial Persona**:

   ○ **Occupation and Role**: Montag is initially presented as a fireman, but in the dystopian world of "Fahrenheit 451," firemen burn books rather than extinguish fires. He is a product of his society, initially proud and unreflective of his role: "It was a pleasure to burn" (Bradbury, Part One).

   ○ **Conformity to Society**: Montag represents the average citizen. He follows the societal norms without question, living a life of routine and superficiality, which is mirrored in his interactions with his wife, Mildred, and his unquestioning acceptance of the state's propaganda.

2. **Transformation Triggered by External Influences**:

   ○ **Impact of Clarisse McClellan**: Clarisse, Montag's teenage neighbor, plays a pivotal role in initiating Montag's transformation. Her curiosity, love for nature, and habit of questioning societal norms intrigue Montag and spark a change in his worldview. She asks him, "Are you happy?" (Bradbury, Part One), a simple question that profoundly impacts Montag, leading him to question his own happiness and purpose.

- **Mildred's Overdose**: The incident of Mildred's attempted suicide and her subsequent lack of memory or concern about it further exacerbates Montag's sense of disillusionment with his life and society.

3. Internal Conflict and Growing Dissent:

- **Awakening to Discontent**: Montag begins to feel a deep sense of unease and dissatisfaction with his life. He becomes increasingly aware of the superficiality and emptiness of his existence and the society around him.

- **Secret Rebellion**: Montag's internal conflict leads him to secretly hoard books, an act of rebellion against the state's anti-book policy. This begins his journey towards seeking knowledge and understanding.

4. Relationships Reflecting his Transformation:

- **Strained Marriage**: Montag's relationship with Mildred, who is deeply immersed in the virtual world of the 'parlor walls' and indifferent to Montag's turmoil, contrasts with his emerging quest for meaning, highlighting the growing chasm between them.

- **Mentorship with Faber**: Montag seeks guidance from Faber, a retired English professor. This relationship is pivotal in Montag's development, as Faber provides intellectual and moral support, aiding Montag's understanding of literature and resistance against societal norms.

5. Climax and Resolution:

- **Rebellion and Pursuit**: Montag's rebellion reaches its zenith when he is forced to burn his own house and subsequently kills Captain Beatty. This act marks the point of no return for Montag and his complete rejection of the oppressive system.

- **Joining the 'Book People'**: In the end, Montag escapes the city and finds solace with the 'Book People,' a group committed to preserving knowledge through memorizing books. This marks Montag's full transformation from a passive censorship enforcer to an active knowledge preserver.

In conclusion, Guy Montag's character arc in "Fahrenheit 451" is a profound exploration of personal awakening and resistance against conformity. His journey from a fireman who burns books to someone who cherishes and preserves them symbolizes the power of individual transformation and the enduring quest for truth and freedom in the face of societal oppression. Montag's character serves as a beacon of hope and a reminder of the resilience of the human spirit.

Describe Clarisse McClellan

Clarisse McClellan is a pivotal character in "Fahrenheit 451," serving as a catalyst for the protagonist Guy Montag's profound transformation. Her character is a beacon of individuality and curiosity in a society marked by conformity and superficiality. Clarisse's unique qualities and perspectives starkly contrast the prevailing norms of the dystopian world Bradbury creates. Here's an in-depth analysis of Clarisse McClellan as a character:

1. **Role and Significance in the Novel**:

   - **Catalyst for Change**: Clarisse is introduced as Montag's seventeen-year-old neighbor. Her inquisitive nature and unconventional views challenge Montag's perceptions and ignite his journey of self-discovery and rebellion against societal norms.

   - **Embodiment of Individuality and Curiosity**: Unlike the majority of characters in the novel, Clarisse indulges in activities that are considered peculiar in their society, like taking long walks, observing the natural world, and engaging in thoughtful conversation.

2. **Character Traits and Philosophy**:

   - **Curiosity and Reflectiveness**: Clarisse is characterized by her curiosity about the world and her desire to explore and understand it deeply. She asks Montag thought-provoking questions, such as "Are you happy?" (Bradbury, Part One), which force him to reflect on his own life and the society they live in.

- **Appreciation for Nature and Human Connection**: Unlike others in her society, Clarisse takes pleasure in the simple joys of nature and human interaction. Her appreciation for these elements highlights what the rest of society lacks due to its obsession with technology and entertainment.

3. Contrast to Other Characters:

- **Antithesis to Mildred**: Clarisse's character is in stark contrast to Mildred, Montag's wife, who epitomizes the empty, disconnected life that most citizens lead. While Mildred is engrossed in the shallow entertainment of their society, Clarisse seeks meaningful experiences and connections.

- **Influence on Montag**: Clarisse's interactions with Montag serve as a mirror that reflects his unexamined life and sparks his transformation. Her questioning nature opens his eyes to the possibility of a different way of living and thinking.

4. Symbolism and Themes:

- **Symbol of Hope and Renewal**: Clarisse represents hope and the potential for renewal in a conformist society. Her presence in the novel symbolizes the enduring power of questioning and critical thinking.

- **Representative of Lost Values**: Clarisse embodies the values and qualities that the society in "Fahrenheit 451" has suppressed or lost, such as curiosity, critical thinking, and appreciation for the natural world.

5. **Clarisse's Mysterious Disappearance**:

- **Impact on Montag**: Clarisse's abrupt disappearance from the novel is a significant moment for Montag. Her presumed death is a turning point that propels him further into his journey of rebellion and search for truth.

- **Enduring Influence**: Despite her short presence in the novel, Clarisse's influence on Montag endures, demonstrating the lasting impact that a single individual can have on another's life and thought process.

In conclusion, Clarisse McClellan's character in "Fahrenheit 451" is a beautifully crafted representation of innocence, curiosity, and non-conformity. Her interactions with Montag play a crucial role in challenging the foundations of the dystopian society depicted in the novel. Through Clarisse, Bradbury effectively illustrates the importance of individual thought, the questioning of societal norms, and the appreciation of the simpler aspects of life that give it meaning and depth. She serves as a reminder of the values that are essential to a full and introspective human experience.

Describe Mildred Montag

Mildred Montag, a pivotal character in "Fahrenheit 451," serves as a stark embodiment of the numbing effects of a conformist and superficial society. Her character is a critical lens through which Bradbury explores themes such as the impact of technology on human relationships and the loss of genuine emotional and intellectual depth. Let's delve into a comprehensive analysis of Mildred Montag:

1. **Role and Representation in the Novel**:

   ○ **Embodiment of Societal Norms**: Mildred represents the average citizen in the dystopian society of "Fahrenheit 451." She is deeply immersed in the superficial entertainment that defines their world, primarily through her obsession with the interactive television 'parlor walls.'

   ○ **Contrast to Guy Montag**: As Montag's wife, Mildred's character is juxtaposed with Montag's growing discontent and quest for meaning. Her indifference and passivity starkly contrast with Montag's emerging critical consciousness and dissatisfaction with their society.

2. **Character Traits and Lifestyle**:

   ○ **Obsession with Technology**: Mildred's life revolves around the 'parlor walls,' large, immersive television screens that dominate her living room. She is more connected to these screens and the fictional characters they display than to the real people in her life, including her husband.

- **Reference**: Mildred's disconnection from reality and her immersion in the virtual world is evident when she describes the 'parlor walls': "My 'family' is people. They tell me things; I laugh, they laugh! And the colors!" (Bradbury, Part One).

3. Emotional and Intellectual Detachment:

- **Lack of Genuine Human Connection**: Mildred's interactions with Montag are characterized by a lack of emotional depth and understanding. She is largely indifferent to Montag's internal struggle and the moral dilemmas he faces.

- **Superficial Existence**: Mildred's life exemplifies the empty existence led by many in their society. Her reliance on sleeping pills and her attempted suicide, which she subsequently cannot remember, underscore the profound emptiness and despair beneath the facade of her technologically saturated life.

4. Representation of Societal Apathy:

- **Indifference to Censorship and Oppression**: Mildred's character illustrates the broader societal apathy toward the censorship and oppression that define their world. She accepts the status quo without question, embodying the passivity and compliance expected by the state.

- **Inability to Recognize Personal Unhappiness**: Despite the superficial comforts of her life, Mildred cannot recognize her own unhappiness or society's oppressive nature, as reflected in her reaction (or lack of) to her own attempted suicide.

5. Mildred's Role in Montag's Transformation:

- **Catalyst for Montag's Change**: While Clarisse sparks Montag's initial questioning of his life and society, his interactions with Mildred and the realization of their empty marriage propel him further on his journey of self-discovery and rebellion.

- **Contrasting Mirror to Montag**: Mildred serves as a mirror to Montag, reflecting what he does not wish to become. Her character highlights the urgency of Montag's quest for meaning and his rejection of the societal values she represents.

In conclusion, Mildred Montag's character in "Fahrenheit 451" is a poignant portrayal of the consequences of a life devoid of authentic emotional and intellectual engagement. Through Mildred, Bradbury effectively illustrates the dehumanizing effects of an overreliance on technology and the dangers of complacency in a society that suppresses individuality and critical thought. Her character stands as a warning against the perils of losing oneself in the superficial pleasures of a technologically dominated world, emphasizing the importance of genuine human connections and introspection.

Describe Captain Beatty

In "Fahrenheit 451," Captain Beatty is a complex and multifaceted character, serving as both an antagonist and a critical voice that elucidates the novel's thematic concerns. As the fire chief and Montag's superior, Beatty represents the oppressive forces of the society, but he also embodies a paradoxical blend of cynicism and insight regarding the world in which they live. Let's explore Captain Beatty's character in detail:

1. **Role and Function in the Narrative**:

   ○ **Antagonist**: Beatty serves as the primary antagonist in the novel. He is a high-ranking official responsible for enforcing the societal ban on books and intellectualism, making him a direct obstacle to Montag's quest for knowledge and freedom.

   ○ **Mentor-like Figure**: Despite being an antagonist, Beatty also plays a mentor-like role for Montag, providing extensive knowledge about the history and rationale behind their society's practices.

2. **Character Traits and Philosophy**:

   ○ **Intelligence and Manipulation**: Beatty is highly intelligent and well-read, which he uses to manipulate and control others, especially Montag. His deep understanding of literature and history is utilized not for enlightenment but to justify the suppression of books.

- **Reference**: Beatty explains to Montag, "If you don't want a man unhappy politically, don't give him two sides to a question to worry him; give him one. Better yet, give him none" (Bradbury, Part One). This quote encapsulates Beatty's cynical view of happiness and knowledge.

- **Cynicism and Contradictions**: Beatty's character is marked by deep cynicism. Despite his understanding of and engagement with literature, he staunchly defends the book-burning policy. This contradiction makes him a complex figure who recognizes the value of what he destroys but believes that censorship is necessary for societal happiness and stability.

3. **Beatty's Interaction with Montag**:

- **Intellectual Confrontations**: Beatty frequently engages Montag in intellectual confrontations, challenging Montag's growing doubts about their society and their work. Through these dialogues, Beatty reveals the internal conflicts and contradictions of the society.

- **Provocateur**: Beatty seems to understand Montag's inner turmoil intuitively and often provokes him, testing his loyalty to the fireman's cause and his adherence to societal norms.

4. **Symbolism of Beatty's Character**:

- **Embodiment of Societal Control**: Beatty symbolizes the oppressive control of the state over individual thought and freedom. His enforcement of book burning and his debates with Montag represent the larger conflict between individuality and conformity.

- ○ **Tragic Understanding**: Beatty's character can be viewed as tragically self-aware. He understands the value of what he destroys but sees no alternative to the status quo, reflecting the despair and resignation of those who recognize the shortcomings of their society but feel powerless to change it.

5. **Beatty's Demise and its Significance**:

- ○ **Confrontation with Montag**: Beatty's demise comes at the hands of Montag, who turns a flamethrower on him. This act marks a turning point for Montag, signifying his complete break from the oppressive regime.

- ○ **Reference**: Beatty's taunting of Montag and his acceptance of his fate: "Go ahead, Montag, kill me" (Bradbury, Part Three), highlights his complex nature - a mix of resignation and provocation.

In conclusion, Captain Beatty's character in "Fahrenheit 451" is a nuanced portrayal of the complexities and contradictions inherent in a society that censors and controls information. His intellectual depth, combined with his role in maintaining societal oppression, makes him a compelling and thought-provoking figure. Beatty's interactions with Montag provide critical insights into the novel's themes, illuminating the dystopian world Bradbury has created. His character raises profound questions about the role of knowledge, the nature of happiness, and the morality of conformity versus rebellion.

Describe Professor Faber

Professor Faber, in "Fahrenheit 451," is a character of significant importance, embodying the values of knowledge, wisdom, and resistance in a society that shuns intellectualism. His role as a guide and mentor to the protagonist, Guy Montag, is crucial in the development of Montag's character and in the progression of the novel's themes. Let's explore the intricacies of Professor Faber's character:

1. **Background and Role in the Story**:

   ○ **Former English Professor**: Faber is a retired English professor, a relic of a bygone era when literature and critical thinking were valued. His background provides him with a deep understanding of literature and its importance to society.

   ○ **Mentor to Montag**: Faber becomes a mentor to Montag, guiding him through his intellectual awakening and aiding in his rebellion against the oppressive societal norms.

2. **Character Traits and Beliefs**:

   ○ **Cautious and Fearful**: Initially, Faber is portrayed as cautious and somewhat fearful, hesitant to take bold actions against the oppressive regime. This cautiousness is a result of the pervasive fear in society and his sense of vulnerability as an intellectual.

   ○ **Wise and Insightful**: Despite his initial fearfulness, Faber is wise and deeply insightful about the nature of their society and the value of literature. He understands the role of books in fostering critical thinking and emotional depth.

- **Reference**: Faber explains to Montag, "It's not books you need, it's some of the things that once were in books. The same things could be in the 'parlor families' today. The same infinite detail and awareness could be projected through the radios and televisors, but are not" (Bradbury, Part Two).

3. **Influence on Montag and the Plot**:

- **Providing Montag with Direction**: Faber provides Montag with a direction and a more profound purpose in his quest for knowledge. He equips Montag with a two-way radio earpiece (the "green bullet") for communication and advises him on how to subvert the firemen's book-burning agenda.

- **Catalyst for Action**: Faber's influence is a catalyst for Montag's transformation into an active rebel. His guidance and support embolden Montag to take significant risks in challenging the status quo.

4. **Symbolic Representation**:

- **Symbol of Lost Intellectualism**: Faber represents the lost intellectualism and cultural depth of their society. He symbolizes what society has lost due to its censorship and anti-intellectual stance.

- **Conscience of the Novel**: In many ways, Faber serves as the conscience of the novel, articulating the moral and philosophical underpinnings of the narrative. He highlights the consequences of a society devoid of introspection and meaningful discourse.

5. Faber's Development and Role in the Conclusion:

○ **Growth in Courage**: As the novel progresses, Faber shows growth in courage, becoming more willing to resist and fight against the societal norms. This change is partly inspired by Montag's bravery and determination.

○ **Reference**: In a conversation with Montag, Faber reflects on the need for action: "I feel I'm doing what I should've done a lifetime ago. For a little while, I'm not afraid. Maybe it's because I'm doing the right thing at last" (Bradbury, Part Three).

In conclusion, Professor Faber's character in "Fahrenheit 451" is essential for his intellectual and moral influence on Montag and his role in articulating the novel's critique of censorship and the neglect of literature and critical thought. Faber represents the lingering spirit of intellectualism and cultural depth in a society that has largely abandoned these values. His interactions with Montag are pivotal in the narrative, providing depth and insight into the novel's exploration of the importance of knowledge, critical thinking, and the courage to challenge oppressive norms.

Minor Characters

In "Fahrenheit 451" by Ray Bradbury, aside from the central characters like Guy Montag, Clarisse McClellan, Mildred Montag, Captain Beatty, and Professor Faber, the novel also features several minor characters. Though not central to the plot, these characters play significant roles in enriching the narrative and reinforcing its themes. Let's delve into these minor characters and their contributions to the novel:

1. **Mildred's Friends: Mrs. Phelps and Mrs. Bowles:**

   - **Role in Society**: They represent the typical citizens of the dystopian society. Engrossed in their shallow, technology-driven lives, they are largely indifferent to the world around them.

   - **Interaction with Montag**: Their interaction with Montag, especially during the scene where he reads poetry to them, highlights the emotional and intellectual void in their lives. This scene underscores the novel's critique of a society devoid of deep thought and genuine emotion.

   - **Significance**: They serve as a contrast to Montag's growing discontent, emphasizing the widespread apathy and conformity in the society.

2. **The Mechanical Hound:**

   - **Not a Character Per Se**: The Mechanical Hound is not a

traditional character but an important element in the novel. It's a robotic enforcer used by the firemen to track down and punish those who defy societal norms.

○ **Symbolism**: It symbolizes the oppressive, technological control exerted by the state over its citizens. The Hound's relentless pursuit of Montag represents the dangers of a society that uses technology to suppress dissent and maintain conformity.

3. Granger:

○ **Leader of the 'Book People'**: Granger is introduced towards the end of the novel as the leader of the 'Book People,' a group dedicated to preserving literature through memorization.

○ **Role and Influence**: He plays a crucial role in Montag's final transformation, offering him a place in their group and a new purpose in life.

○ **Philosophical Insight**: Granger provides philosophical insight into the importance of knowledge and the human experience, emphasizing the value of what they are doing. He discusses the phoenix and the cyclical nature of human civilization, adding depth to the theme of rebirth and hope.

4. Stoneman and Black:

○ **Fellow Firemen**: Stoneman and Black are Montag's colleagues at the firehouse. They are typical firemen who follow orders without questioning the morality of their actions.

○ **Representative of Conformity**: Their characters represent the faceless masses who conform to the dictates of their society without reflection. They highlight Montag's growing alienation from his peers and job.

5. **The Old Woman**:

- ○ **Defiant Book Owner**: The old woman is a pivotal minor character who chooses to burn along with her books rather than live in a world without them.

- ○ **Impact on Montag**: Her act of defiance and her willingness to die for her books profoundly affect Montag, accelerating his disillusionment with his role as a fireman and the society in which he lives.

- ○ **Symbol of Resistance**: She symbolizes the ultimate resistance to censorship and the oppressive regime, emphasizing the novel's themes of the power of literature and the human spirit.

Though these minor characters occupy less narrative space, they contribute significantly to the thematic richness and depth of "Fahrenheit 451." They provide context and contrast to the protagonist's journey, enrich the portrayal of the dystopian society, and underscore the novel's exploration of censorship, conformity, and the value of intellectual freedom. Through these characters, Bradbury creates a vivid tapestry that captures the complexities of his imagined world and the struggles within it.

Important Relationships

"Fahrenheit 451" features several important relationships that play crucial roles in the development of the narrative and its themes. Each relationship illuminates different aspects of the characters and the society in which they live. Here's an in-depth look at these relationships:

1. **Guy Montag and Clarisse McClellan:**

   - **Nature of Relationship**: Clarisse, a young and curious neighbor, represents a stark contrast to the conformist society. Her relationship with Montag is one of mentorship and inspiration. She is not romantically involved with Montag but plays a pivotal role in awakening his curiosity and questioning nature.

   - **Impact on Montag**: Clarisse's innocent questions and her appreciation for the natural world and human connection ignite a change in Montag. She prompts him to question the society's norms and his own happiness and role within it.

   - **Reference**: Clarisse's simple yet profound question, "Are you happy?" (Bradbury, Part One), serves as a catalyst for Montag's transformation.

2. **Guy Montag and Mildred Montag:**

   - **Nature of Relationship**: Mildred, Montag's wife, is deeply immersed in the shallow culture of their society. Their marriage is depicted as emotionally distant and disconnected.

○ **Contrast in Values**: Mildred's obsession with the 'parlor walls' and indifference to Montag's inner turmoil accentuate their growing rift. Their relationship serves as a microcosm of the larger societal issues of isolation and superficiality.

○ **Reference**: Mildred's apathy is evident when she dismisses Montag's growing concerns: "You need to rest. Forget about the firemen, forget about the books" (Bradbury, Part One).

3. Guy Montag and Captain Beatty:

○ **Nature of Relationship**: Beatty, the fire chief, initially serves as a mentor to Montag. However, as Montag's views begin to change, their relationship becomes antagonistic.

○ **Intellectual and Ideological Conflict**: Beatty is aware of Montag's internal conflict and challenges him intellectually. He uses his own knowledge of literature to justify the burning of books and to maintain control over Montag.

○ **Reference**: Beatty's confrontational speech to Montag: "We must all be alike. Not everyone born free and equal, as the Constitution says, but everyone made equal" (Bradbury, Part One), reveals the depth of their ideological divide.

4. Guy Montag and Professor Faber:

○ **Nature of Relationship**: Faber, a retired English professor, becomes a mentor and ally to Montag. He represents the intellectualism and knowledge that Montag seeks.

- **Guidance and Support**: Faber aids Montag in his quest for understanding and provides practical assistance in his rebellion against societal norms. Their relationship is based on mutual respect and a shared commitment to preserving knowledge.

- **Reference**: Faber's guidance is crucial to Montag's plan: "I'll give you a few lines from your part every day and you can try them out on your friends and see what they say" (Bradbury, Part Two).

5. Guy Montag and the 'Book People':

- **Nature of Relationship**: The 'Book People' are a group of individuals Montag encounters after fleeing the city. They are dedicated to preserving the knowledge in books by memorizing them.

- **Symbol of Hope and Resistance**: This group represents a new beginning for Montag. Their commitment to preserving literature symbolizes hope for a future where intellectual freedom is valued.

- **Reference**: The leader of the 'Book People,' Granger, explains their mission: "We're remembering" (Bradbury, Part Three), indicating a collective effort to resist the oppressive societal norms.

In conclusion, the relationships in "Fahrenheit 451" are instrumental in exploring and advancing the novel's themes of conformity, censorship, intellectual freedom, and the search for meaning. Each relationship challenges or supports Montag in different ways, contributing to his transformation and the overall narrative arc. Through these relationships, Brad-

bury highlights the importance of human connection, intellectual curiosity, and moral courage in a society that often discourages such qualities.

Guy Montag and Clarisse McClellan

The relationship between Guy Montag and Clarisse McClellan in "Fahrenheit 451" is pivotal to the narrative and serves as a catalyst for Montag's transformation. This relationship, though brief in the span of the novel, is deeply significant in its impact on Montag's character and his view of the world. Let's explore this relationship in more detail:

1. **Nature and Dynamics of the Relationship**:

   - **Mentorship and Inspiration**: Clarisse, a young, inquisitive neighbor, serves more as a mentor or muse to Montag rather than a romantic interest. Her free-spirited nature, curiosity about the world, and penchant for deep questions starkly contrast with Montag's initial complacency.

   - **Intellectual and Emotional Awakening**: Clarisse's conversations with Montag spark his intellectual and emotional awakening. She challenges him to look at the world differently and question their society's norms.

2. **Impact on Montag**:

   - **Catalyst for Change**: Clarisse's influence on Montag is profound. Her simple yet thoughtful questions, such as "Are you happy?" (Bradbury, Part One), force Montag to introspect and confront his own dissatisfaction and the superficiality of his existence.

○ **Seeing the World Anew**: Through Clarisse's eyes, Montag begins to notice aspects of the world he had previously ignored. She teaches him to appreciate the beauty in nature, the joy of conversation, and the value of being present in the moment.

3. Contrast to Montag's Life:

○ **Different Perspectives**: Clarisse represents everything that Montag's life with Mildred is not. While Mildred is absorbed in the shallow entertainment of their society, Clarisse is reflective, appreciative of nature, and seeks meaningful connections.

○ **Opening Montag's Eyes**: Clarisse's behavior, such as her enjoyment of rain, her observation of the moon, and her participation in seemingly trivial but profound activities, opens Montag's eyes to a different way of living and thinking.

4. Clarisse as a Symbol of Hope:

○ **Embodiment of Freedom and Individuality**: Clarisse symbolizes the possibility of a free, thoughtful, and fulfilling life, contrary to the oppressive norms of their society. She is a breath of fresh air in a stifling environment, embodying the hope for a better, more enlightened world.

○ **Lasting Influence**: Clarisse's presence in the novel is short-lived, but her impact on Montag lasts. She sets him on a path of self-discovery and rebellion against societal constraints.

5. Montag's Transformation Post-Clarisse:

○ **Quest for Knowledge**: Inspired by Clarisse, Montag begins to question not just his fireman job but also the foundations of his society. He seeks knowledge and truth, which leads him to the illegal act of hoarding and reading books.

○ **Change in Montag's Character**: The relationship with Clarisse marks the beginning of Montag's transformation from a conforming citizen to a questioning, rebellious individual. It ignites a spark in him that drives the rest of his journey in the novel.

In conclusion, the relationship between Guy Montag and Clarisse McClellan is a key element of "Fahrenheit 451." Clarisse's influence on Montag is the catalyst for his dramatic character development. She opens his mind and heart to the possibilities of a life filled with curiosity, beauty, and meaning, setting him on a course that ultimately leads to his rebellion against the societal status quo. Though brief, her role in the novel is integral to its narrative and thematic development.

Chapter 35

Guy Montag and Mildred Montag

The relationship between Guy Montag and his wife, Mildred Montag, in "Fahrenheit 451" is a critical element of the narrative, reflecting the broader themes of disconnection, escapism, and the impact of an oppressive society on personal relationships. Their marriage serves as a microcosm of Bradbury's dystopian world, illustrating the emotional and intellectual void created by a culture obsessed with superficial entertainment and devoid of genuine human connection. Let's explore this relationship in more detail:

1. **Emotional and Intellectual Disconnection**:

   ○ **Lack of Genuine Communication**: Guy and Mildred's relationship is characterized by a profound lack of communication and emotional connection. Their interactions are superficial and devoid of the depth and understanding that typify a healthy relationship.

   ○ **Reference**: Mildred's obsession with the 'parlor walls' and her indifference to Montag's growing unease reflect this disconnection: "He felt that the room was full of ghosts" (Bradbury, Part One).

2. **Contrasting Values and Perspectives**:

- **Mildred's Escapism**: Mildred represents the archetypical citizen of their society, completely absorbed in the shallow entertainment provided by the 'parlor walls' and indifferent to the reality around her. She finds her solace and meaning in the virtual world of her TV 'family,' ignoring both her husband's struggles and the larger societal issues.

- **Montag's Quest for Meaning**: As Montag begins to question the society's norms and seeks deeper meaning in life, the chasm between him and Mildred widens. His growing interest in books and the world of ideas stands in stark contrast to Mildred's apathy and escapism.

3. **Mildred as a Product of Society**:

- **Reflective of Societal Norms**: Mildred's character is a reflection of the societal values promoted by the government in "Fahrenheit 451." Her addiction to the 'parlor walls' and her attempted suicide, which she subsequently forgets or denies, highlight the profound emptiness and despair beneath the façade of her technologically saturated life.

- **Reference**: Mildred's lack of memory or concern about her own attempted suicide underscores the deep malaise affecting individuals in the society: "Mildred, don't you remember?" (Bradbury, Part One).

4. Impact on Montag's Transformation:

- **Catalyst for Rebellion**: While Clarisse sparks Montag's initial questioning of his life, his interactions with Mildred and the realization of their empty marriage propel him further into his journey of self-discovery and rebellion against societal norms.

- **Reference**: The stark contrast between Montag's emerging awareness and Mildred's obliviousness to the world is a recurring theme in their interactions: "He felt as if he had left a stage behind and many actors" (Bradbury, Part Three).

5. Symbolism of Their Relationship:

- **Symbol of Societal Decay**: The Montags' relationship symbolizes the broader decay of human connection and values in their society. Their marriage is a casualty of a culture that values entertainment over intimacy and distraction over depth.

- **Reference**: The scene where Montag reads poetry to Mildred and her friends, only to be met with confusion and hostility, symbolizes the chasm between those seeking meaning and those content with the superficiality of their society: "He read a dozen pages here or there and came at last to this: 'It was a pleasure to burn'" (Bradbury, Part Two).

In conclusion, the relationship between Guy Montag and Mildred Montag is a poignant portrayal of the dehumanizing effects of a society that suppresses individual thought and emotion in favor of conformity and superficial entertainment. Through their failing marriage, Bradbury explores themes of alienation, the loss of individuality, and the consequences of living in a society that discourages genuine human connection and intellectual curiosity. Their relationship warns against the dangers of disconnection from self and others, emphasizing the need for emotional and intellectual engagement in a meaningful life.

GUY MONTAG AND CAPTAIN BEATTY

The relationship between Guy Montag and Captain Beatty in "Fahrenheit 451" is complex and fraught with tension, encapsulating several of the novel's key themes, such as censorship, rebellion, and the conflict between individualism and authority. This relationship evolves significantly over the course of the narrative and is central to Montag's transformation. Let's delve deeper into the nuances of their relationship:

Initial Relationship - Mentorship and Authority:

1. **Beatty as a Mentor**: In the early stages of the novel, Captain Beatty, as Montag's boss and the fire chief, assumes a role akin to a mentor. He is knowledgeable, articulate, and seemingly understanding of Montag's initial confusion and curiosity.

2. **Respect and Authority**: Montag initially respects Beatty as an authority figure and values his wisdom. Despite his role in burning books, Beatty's extensive knowledge of literature adds complexity to his character and relationship with Montag.

3. **Reference**: Beatty's articulation of the societal norms and justification for book burning initially helps to assuage Montag's doubts: "We stand against the small tide of those who want to make everyone unhappy with conflicting theory and thought" (Bradbury, Part One).

Emergence of Conflict and Ideological Clash:

1. **Montag's Growing Doubts**: As Montag becomes increasingly disillusioned with his role as a fireman and the society's censorship, his relationship with Beatty becomes strained. Montag starts to see Beatty not just as a mentor but as a symbol of the oppressive system he serves.

2. **Beatty's Awareness and Manipulation**: Beatty, perceptive and cunning, senses Montag's growing discontent and attempts to manipulate him. He uses his knowledge of books to intimidate and control Montag, revealing a more sinister aspect of his character.

3. **Reference**: Beatty's monologues to Montag, where he explains the history of their society and the justification for its current state, become increasingly manipulative: "You must understand that our civilization is so vast that we can't have our minorities upset and stirred" (Bradbury, Part One).

Climactic Confrontation and Resolution:

1. **Confrontation and Revelation**: The relationship culminates in a dramatic confrontation at Montag's home. Beatty forces Montag to burn his own house, symbolizing Montag's final break from the society and his role in it.

2. **Beatty as Antagonist**: In this climactic scene, Beatty becomes the clear antagonist, taunting Montag and pushing him to a breaking point. This confrontation is not just between two individuals but represents the broader battle between individual freedom and authoritarian control.

3. **Reference**: The intensity of their conflict reaches its peak when

Montag turns the flamethrower on Beatty, an act of both desperation and defiance: "Beatty wanted to die...He just stood there, not really trying to save himself" (Bradbury, Part Three).

Symbolic Significance:

1. **Symbol of Oppression and Rebellion**: Their relationship symbolizes the broader thematic conflicts in the novel. Beatty represents the oppressive force of the government and societal conformity, while Montag comes to embody individual rebellion and the pursuit of knowledge.

2. **Reference**: Beatty's final moments, where he accepts his fate at the hands of Montag, symbolize the inevitable clash between oppressive authority and the human desire for freedom and truth.

In conclusion, the relationship between Guy Montag and Captain Beatty in "Fahrenheit 451" is a dynamic and symbolically charged aspect of the narrative. It evolves from one of mentorship and respect to one of conflict and rebellion, mirroring Montag's own transformation. Through this relationship, Bradbury explores the complexities of power, control, and the individual's struggle against an oppressive society. The relationship serves as a vehicle for the novel's exploration of themes related to censorship, the value of knowledge, and the importance of questioning authority.

Guy Montag and Professor Faber

The relationship between Guy Montag and Professor Faber in "Fahrenheit 451" is a key element of the novel, embodying the themes of intellectual curiosity, mentorship, and the fight against censorship. This relationship is instrumental in Montag's transformation from a compliant fireman to a questioning rebel. Let's examine the nuances of their relationship in more detail:

1. **Faber as a Mentor and Guide**:

   ○ **Meeting and Initial Interaction**: Montag first encounters Faber, a retired English professor, when he is at the peak of his internal conflict about the society's ban on books. Faber represents the intellectualism and knowledge that Montag craves but lacks.

   ○ **Influence on Montag**: Faber significantly influences Montag's development, providing him with deeper insights into literature and the importance of ideas. Faber's guidance helps Montag understand what he is fighting for – preserving and disseminating knowledge.

2. **Development of Their Relationship**:

   ○ **Shared Love for Books**: Their relationship is built on mutual respect for and interest in books and what they represent. Faber provides Montag with the intellectual and emotional support he needs to challenge the status quo.

- **Collaborative Effort Against Censorship**: Faber and Montag form a partnership to defy the societal norms and censorship laws. Faber uses his knowledge to aid Montag's rebellion, devising plans to undermine the firemen's authority and spread the word about books.

3. **Faber's Role in Montag's Rebellion**:

- **Providing Tools and Tactics**: Faber gives Montag a two-way communication device (the green bullet) to stay in contact, symbolizing their connection and the merging of their efforts. This tool is crucial in several of Montag's actions against the firemen.

- **Cautious Approach**: Faber's cautious nature contrasts with Montag's impulsiveness, highlighting the practical and strategic aspects of rebellion. He advises Montag on how to act and provides a more pragmatic perspective on their fight against censorship.

4. **Impact on Montag's Transformation**:

- **Intellectual Awakening**: Faber plays a crucial role in Montag's intellectual awakening. He helps Montag to see beyond the physical aspect of books and understand their content's significance in preserving human experiences and thoughts.

- **Reference**: Faber explains the importance of books to Montag: "The magic is only in what books say, how they stitched the patches of the universe together into one garment for us" (Bradbury, Part Two).

5. **Faber's Own Growth and Change**:

- **From Fear to Action**: Faber's relationship with Montag also influences his own character. Initially fearful and hesitant to act against the oppressive society, Faber grows bolder and more willing to take risks as he becomes more involved with Montag.

- **Reference**: Faber's decision to join forces with Montag and plan their rebellion marks a significant shift in his character from a fearful recluse to an active participant in the resistance.

6. **Symbolic Significance of Their Relationship**:

- **Connection Between Knowledge and Action**: The relationship between Montag and Faber symbolizes the connection between knowledge and action. It demonstrates that intellectual understanding needs to be coupled with practical action to effect change.

- **Interplay of Youth and Experience**: Their partnership represents the interplay of youth and experience, impulsiveness and caution, action and wisdom, highlighting the multidimensional nature of rebellion against oppression.

In conclusion, the relationship between Guy Montag and Professor Faber in "Fahrenheit 451" is crucial to developing the novel's plot and articulating its themes. Through this relationship, Bradbury explores the power of mentorship, the importance of intellectual courage, and the dynamics of resistance in a society that suppresses free thought. Montag and Faber's partnership illustrates how knowledge and action can come together to challenge and subvert oppressive societal norms.

Imagery, Symbols and Alegory

In "Fahrenheit 451," Ray Bradbury masterfully employs imagery, symbols, and allegory to enhance the novel's thematic depth and emotional resonance. These literary devices enrich the reader's experience and underscore the critical commentary on society, technology, and human nature. Let's explore these elements in detail:

Imagery

1. **Fire and Flames**:

   ○ **Destructive and Purifying**: The imagery of fire is multifaceted in the novel. Initially, it symbolizes destruction, censorship, and the oppressive power of the state: "It was a pleasure to burn. It was a special pleasure to see things eaten, to see things blackened and changed" (Bradbury, Part One). However, as the novel progresses, fire also comes to represent knowledge, enlightenment, and the possibility of rebirth. The dual nature of fire reflects the complex relationship between destruction and renewal.

   ○ **Montag's Fascination with Fire**: Montag's changing perception of fire mirrors his transformation. Early in the novel, he is mesmerized by the destructive beauty of flames, but later, he comes to see fire as a source of warmth and a symbol of human connection and hope, particularly in the context of the 'Book People.'

2. **The Mechanical Hound**:

○ **Technological Menace**: The Mechanical Hound is vividly described as a menacing and dehumanized technological creation. Its imagery evokes fear and serves as a representation of the state's cold, mechanical control over individuals. The Hound's injections and its relentless tracking abilities make it a symbol of the pervasive and invasive nature of the oppressive government.

○ **Contrast to Natural Imagery**: The unnatural, mechanical imagery of the Hound starkly contrasts with the more organic and human elements in the novel, underscoring the theme of technological domination over human values.

3. **The River and Nature**:

○ **Escape and Transformation**: The imagery associated with the river and nature represents escape and transformation. When Montag flees the city, the river is described in a way that evokes a sense of cleansing and renewal. The natural surroundings contrast with the oppressive, artificial environment of the city, symbolizing Montag's journey towards freedom and enlightenment.

○ **Sensory Experience**: Bradbury's descriptions of the natural world are rich in sensory details, offering a respite from the oppressive atmosphere of the city. The tranquility and beauty of nature provide a backdrop for Montag's introspection and growth.

4. The 'Parlor Walls' and the Seashell Radios:

○ **Sensory Overload and Superficiality**: The imagery of the 'parlor walls' and the Seashell radios in Mildred's world is one of sensory overload. The loud, continuous, and overwhelming broadcasts represent their society's superficiality and sensory bombardment. This imagery highlights the contrast between the shallow distractions of technology and the depth of real human experience.

○ **Isolation and Disconnection**: The vivid descriptions of Mildred and others being absorbed by these devices emphasize the disconnection and isolation fostered by technology.

5. Imagery of Ash and Dust:

○ **Decay and Loss**: The novel's recurrent imagery of ash and dust symbolizes decay, loss, and the erasure of identity. This imagery often surrounds the firemen's work, reflecting the destruction of culture and history that their actions represent.

○ **Reference**: "He was a thing of brush and powder, like the women down the hall" (Bradbury, Part One), describing Montag after a night of burning, evoking a sense of emptiness and impermanence.

Through imagery, Bradbury explores themes of destruction and renewal, the perils of technological advancement, the power of nature, and the human quest for knowledge and freedom. The imagery not only serves to create a visually compelling narrative but also deepens the reader's understanding of the novel's complex themes and emotional landscape.

Symbols

These symbols are not mere literary devices; they serve as integral components of the story, offering deeper insights into the characters' experiences and their dystopian world. Let's explore these symbols in greater depth:

1. **Books**:

   ○ **Representing Knowledge and Freedom**: Books are the most prominent symbol in the novel. They represent knowledge, freedom of thought, and the power of ideas. In a society where books are banned, possessing and reading them become acts of rebellion and self-assertion.

   ○ **Symbol of Individuality and Diversity**: Each book is unique and offers different perspectives, symbolizing the diversity of human thought and the richness of individual experiences.

   ○ **Reference**: When Montag discovers the beauty and complexity of books, he realizes their value, "He opened the book to read: 'It was a pleasure to burn'" (Bradbury, Part One). This ironic moment highlights the transition from ignorance to awareness.

2. **The Mechanical Hound**:

   ○ **Technological Control and Suppression**: The Mechanical Hound symbolizes the oppressive power of the state and the use of technology to control and suppress individual freedom. Its relentless pursuit of dissenters is emblematic of the government's determination to eliminate any form of resistance.

- **Dehumanization**: The Hound, with its lack of organic qualities and programmed behavior, represents the dehumanization inherent in a technology-dominated society.

- **Reference**: "The Hound leaped up into the air with a rhythm and a sense of smell of a machine" (Bradbury, Part One), emphasizing its mechanical and emotionless nature.

3. Fire:

- **Destruction and Renewal**: Fire symbolizes both destruction and renewal. Initially, it represents the destructive power of censorship, as firemen burn books to suppress knowledge. However, as Montag's perception changes, fire also comes to symbolize warmth, enlightenment, and the potential for a new beginning.

- **Reference**: "He saw himself in her eyes, suspended in two shining drops of bright water, himself dark and tiny, in fine detail, the lines about his mouth, everything there, as if her eyes were two miraculous bits of violet amber that might capture and hold him intact" (Bradbury, Part One). This imagery reflects Montag's transformation and the duality of fire.

4. The Phoenix:

- **Cycle of Destruction and Rebirth**: The Phoenix is a mythological bird that is reborn from its ashes. In the novel, it symbolizes the cyclical nature of human civilization – destruction followed by rebirth.

- **Reference**: Captain Beatty refers to the Phoenix, "There was a silly damn bird called a Phoenix back before Christ, every few hundred years he built a pyre and burnt himself up" (Brad-bury, Part One). This allusion to the Phoenix foretells the eventual destruction and hoped-for rebirth of society.

5. **The Sieve and the Sand**:

   ◦ **Futility and the Elusiveness of Knowledge**: The title of the second part of the novel, "The Sieve and the Sand," is a symbol derived from Montag's childhood memory. It represents the futility of trying to fill a sieve with sand, paralleling Montag's struggle to comprehend and retain the knowledge he gains from books.

   ◦ **Reference**: Montag's recollection of the sieve and the sand symbolizes his deep desire for knowledge and his frustration with the elusive nature of truth in a society steeped in censorship.

Expanding further on the symbols in "Fahrenheit 451," we uncover deeper layers of meaning that contribute significantly to the novel's thematic richness. Bradbury's symbols are vivid and memorable and carry profound implications about society, human nature, and the struggle between conformity and individuality. Let's explore additional dimensions of the key symbols in the novel:

1. **Books as Symbols of Individual Thought and Resistance**:

   ◦ **Contrast with Mass Media**: Books symbolize the antithesis of the mass media culture depicted in the novel. While the 'parlor walls' promote passive consumption and conformity, books represent active engagement, critical thinking, and diversity of perspectives.

- **Reference**: "A book is a loaded gun in the house next d oor...Who knows who might be the target of the well-read man?" (Bradbury, Part One). This metaphor underscores the perceived threat that books pose to the society in the novel, representing individual empowerment and intellectual freedom.

2. **The Mechanical Hound as a Symbol of Technological Domination**:

- **Control and Surveillance**: The Mechanical Hound symbolizes state control and broader themes of surveillance and technological overreach. It represents a society where technological advancements are used to suppress, rather than empower, individuals.

- **Reference**: "The Hound was gone now... Its kennel was empty and the firehouse stood all about in plaster silence" (Bradbury, Part One). The Hound's presence and subsequent absence illustrate the pervasive yet unseen threat of technological control.

3. **Fire as a Symbol of Dualities**:

- **Destruction and Enlightenment**: Fire's dual symbolism in the novel is multifaceted. It represents both the destructive force used by the totalitarian regime to suppress dissent and a tool of enlightenment and warmth for those who seek knowledge and truth.

- **Reference**: "He felt as if he had left a stage behind and many actors. He felt as if he had left the great séance and all the murmuring ghosts. He was moving from an unreality that was

frightening into a reality that was unreal because it was new"
(Bradbury, Part Three). This transition signifies the shift in
Montag's perception of fire from destruction to renewal.

4. **The Phoenix as a Symbol of Renewal and Cyclical History**:

○ **Endurance and Rebirth**: The Phoenix symbol is crucial in
understanding the novel's perspective on history and humanity's capacity for renewal. It suggests that destruction is not
absolute but part of a cycle that can lead to rebirth and change.

○ **Reference**: "There was a silly damn bird called a Phoenix
back before Christ: every few hundred years he built a pyre
and burnt himself up...but every time he burnt himself up he
sprang out of the ashes, he got himself born all over again"
(Bradbury, Part One). This reference by Beatty highlights the
cyclical nature of destruction and rebirth, paralleling Montag's
own transformation.

5. **The Sieve and the Sand as a Symbol of Futility and Persis-
tence**:

○ **Search for Meaning**: The symbol of the sieve and the sand
represents Montag's quest for knowledge and the frustration
that comes with trying to grasp something elusive. It symbolizes the difficulty of obtaining and retaining truth in a world
filled with distractions and superficiality.

○ **Reference**: "He wore his happiness like a mask and the girl had
run off across the lawn with the mask and there was no way of
going to knock on her door and ask for it back" (Bradbury, Part
Two). This metaphor reflects Montag's struggle to internalize
and comprehend the information he encounters, akin to the

futility of filling a sieve with sand.

The symbols in "Fahrenheit 451" are powerful tools that Bradbury uses to deepen the novel's exploration of its themes. Books, the Mechanical Hound, fire, the Phoenix, and the sieve and the sand serve not just as narrative elements but as reflections of the characters' struggles and the societal issues the novel addresses. Through these symbols, Bradbury invites readers to ponder the complexities of knowledge, freedom, and the human experience in a world where conformity and ignorance are the norms.

Allegory

Ray Bradbury crafts a multifaceted allegory transcending its immediate narrative to offer profound commentary on broader societal issues. The novel's allegorical elements critique mid-20th-century America, but their relevance extends to contemporary concerns about censorship, media saturation, and the loss of critical thinking.

1. **Allegory of Censorship and Intellectual Oppression**:

   ○ **Suppression of Books and Ideas**: The government's censorship of books in the novel allegorically represents the dangers of suppressing dissenting ideas and perspectives. This is reflective of historical periods where authoritarian regimes sought to control knowledge to maintain power.

   ○ **Reference**: Captain Beatty's explanation of the history of book burning provides insight into this allegory: "It didn't come from the Government down. There was no dictum, no declaration, no censorship, to start with, no! Technology, mass exploitation, and minority pressure carried the trick" (Bradbury, Part One).

2. **Allegory of the Dangers of Mass Media and Technology**:

○ **The 'Parlor Walls' and Seashell Radios**: These technologies in the novel symbolize the numbing effects of media and technology on the populace. They serve as an allegory for how television, radio, and, by extension, modern social media can create a passive, unthinking society, distracted from more meaningful engagement with the world.

○ **Reference**: Mildred's addiction to her 'parlor family' and the constant noise of the Seashell radios exemplify this: "And in her ears the little Seashells, the thimble radios tamped tight, and an electronic ocean of sound" (Bradbury, Part One).

3. **Allegory of the Role of Intellectualism and Education**:

○ **Value of Knowledge and Critical Thinking**: The novel allegorizes the importance of intellectualism and education in maintaining a free and thoughtful society. The 'Book People' at the end of the novel represent the preservation of knowledge as a bulwark against ignorance and tyranny.

○ **Reference**: Granger's discussion with Montag about their role in preserving knowledge underscores this: "We're remembering" (Bradbury, Part Three).

4. **Allegory of Conformity vs. Individuality**:

○ **Society's Conformity**: The novel's society, where dissent and difference are suppressed, serves as an allegory for the dangers of societal conformity. It reflects concerns about the loss of individuality in the face of overwhelming societal pressure to conform.

- ○ **Reference**: Montag's transformation from a conforming fireman to a questioning rebel is symbolic of the struggle for individuality: "He was not empty. There was more than enough here to fill him" (Bradbury, Part Three).

5. **Allegory of Complacency and Resistance**:

- ○ **Societal Apathy**: The widespread indifference in the novel's society allegorizes the dangers of public complacency in the face of governmental overreach and cultural decline.

- ○ **Resistance as a Duty**: Montag's eventual rebellion symbolizes the moral duty to resist oppressive norms and to seek truth, even in the face of personal risk.

- ○ **Reference**: Montag's realization of his role in perpetuating the system and his subsequent rebellion highlights this allegorical element: "I can't talk to my wife; she listens to the walls" (Bradbury, Part Two).

"Fahrenheit 451" is a rich allegory that explores themes of censorship, technology, conformity, intellectualism, and resistance. Through its narrative, Bradbury warns of the perils of a society that forsakes intellectual freedom and critical thought for the sake of comfort and conformity. The novel serves as a timeless reminder of the importance of safeguarding these values to preserve the essence of a free and vibrant society.

CONFLICTS

"Fahrenheit 451" is a novel rich with conflicts that drive its narrative and underlying themes. These conflicts are both external and internal, portraying the struggles of individuals against a repressive society and their internal battles with their own beliefs and identities. Let's examine these conflicts in detail:

1. **Individual vs. Society**:

   ○ **Montag vs. The Dystopian Society**: The primary conflict in the novel is between Montag and the dystopian society in which he lives. Montag's growing dissatisfaction with a society that bans books and discourages intellectualism puts him at odds with the government and its oppressive norms.

   ○ **Reference**: Montag's internal struggle becomes external when he starts hoarding books, an act of rebellion against the state's anti-book policy: "He could feel the firehouse full of glitter and shine; and himself, sitting there, waiting for the next alarm, for the next fire" (Bradbury, Part One).

2. **Man vs. Technology**:

   ○ **Montag and Society vs. The Mechanical Hound**: A significant conflict in the novel is between the characters (especially Montag) and the Mechanical Hound, a symbol of technological control and oppression. The Hound's pursuit of

Montag represents the larger battle against a society that uses technology to suppress individual thought and freedom.

○ **Reference**: The Hound's relentless pursuit of Montag, leading to a dramatic confrontation, illustrates this conflict: "The Hound leaped up into the air with a rhythm and a sense of smell of a machine" (Bradbury, Part One).

3. Individual vs. Self:

○ **Montag's Internal Conflict**: Montag experiences a profound internal conflict between his ingrained beliefs as a fireman and his emerging doubts about the society's values. His transformation from a conformist to a questioner is at the heart of the novel.

○ **Reference**: Montag's introspection and doubt are evident when he contemplates the content and meaning of books: "There must be something in books, things we can't imagine, to make a woman stay in a burning house; there must be something there. You don't stay for nothing" (Bradbury, Part One).

4. Individual vs. Authority:

○ **Montag vs. Captain Beatty**: Montag's conflict with Captain Beatty represents his struggle against the authoritative figures who enforce the society's repressive laws. As Montag's fire chief and the novel's antagonist, Beatty embodies the values and beliefs that Montag comes to question and oppose.

○ **Reference**: The intellectual and ideological confrontations between Montag and Beatty highlight this conflict: "We must all be alike. Not everyone born free and equal, as the Constitution says, but everyone made equal" (Bradbury, Part One), Beatty's justification of their society's principles.

5. **Society vs. Intellectualism**:

○ **Societal Suppression of Knowledge**: A significant theme is the conflict between a society that suppresses intellectualism and the inherent human desire for knowledge and truth. This conflict is embodied in the firemen's burning of books and the existence of 'Book People' who memorize books to preserve knowledge.

○ **Reference**: The existence and role of the 'Book People' at the end of the novel symbolize the resistance to societal oppression of intellectualism: "We're remembering" (Bradbury, Part Three).

In conclusion, the conflicts in "Fahrenheit 451" are integral to its narrative and thematic exploration. They provide a dynamic framework through which Bradbury examines issues of censorship, conformity, individuality, and the role of technology in society. These conflicts drive the novel's plot and contribute to the development of its characters, especially Montag, whose journey is marked by a series of confrontations that challenge his beliefs and ultimately lead to his transformation. Through these conflicts, Bradbury invites readers to reflect on the importance of intellectual freedom and the dangers of complacency in the face of authoritarianism.

Individual vs. Society

The conflict between the individual and society in "Fahrenheit 451" is a central theme that drives the novel's narrative and underlines its critical commentary on conformity, censorship, and the suppression of intellectual freedom. This conflict is primarily embodied in the character of Guy Montag and his transformation from a conformist fireman to a questioning individual. Let's expand on this conflict in detail:

1. **Montag's Role in Society**:

   - **Initial Conformity**: At the start, Montag is a typical product of his society. As a fireman, he is an active participant in the state's censorship regime, burning books and perpetuating the ignorance that the government mandates. His role symbolizes the society's collective ethos of conformity and anti-intellectualism.

   - **Reference**: Montag's initial pride in his work: "It was a pleasure to burn" (Bradbury, Part One), highlights his initial alignment with societal norms.

2. **Societal Suppression and Control**:

   - **Censorship and Intellectual Oppression**: The society in "Fahrenheit 451" exerts control over individuals primarily through censorship and the suppression of books, which are the repositories of diverse ideas and free thought. This represents a broader conflict between individual curiosity and societal suppression.

○ **Technological Manipulation**: The state also uses technology, like the 'parlor walls' and the Mechanical Hound, to maintain control over its citizens, ensuring they remain passive consumers of shallow entertainment rather than active, thinking individuals.

○ **Reference**: Captain Beatty's explanation of the firemen's role and the history of censorship reflects this societal control: "We stand against the small tide of those who want to make everyone unhappy with conflicting theory and thought" (Bradbury, Part One).

3. **Montag's Awakening and Rebellion**:

○ **Influence of Clarisse and Books**: Montag's encounter with Clarisse McClellan sparks his transformation. Her questions and unconventional outlook prompt him to reflect on his own life and the society around him. His subsequent secret accumulation of books signifies his growing resistance to societal norms.

○ **Internal Conflict**: Montag's burgeoning curiosity and doubt place him in direct conflict with his society's values. This internal struggle is a microcosm of the broader battle between individual enlightenment and societal conformity.

○ **Reference**: Montag's turmoil and emerging dissent: "There must be something in books, things we can't imagine, to make a woman stay in a burning house; there must be something there. You don't stay for nothing" (Bradbury, Part One).

4. Climactic Confrontation with Society:

- ○ **Montag vs. The Firemen and Beatty**: The climax of Montag's conflict with society occurs when he is forced to burn his own home and subsequently kills Beatty. This act is both literal and symbolic, representing his final break with the oppressive norms of his society.

- ○ **Reference**: The confrontation between Montag and Beatty is a pivotal moment in this conflict: "Montag only said, 'We never burned right...'" (Bradbury, Part Three), illustrating his complete rejection of societal values.

5. Montag's Escape and Future Hope:

- ○ **Joining the 'Book People'**: Montag's escape and joining the 'Book People' represent a resolution to his conflict with society. He finds hope in a group of individuals committed to preserving knowledge, indicating the possibility of a future society where individual thought is valued.

- ○ **Reference**: Montag's new beginning with the 'Book People': "And when the war's over, some day, some year, the books can be written again..." (Bradbury, Part Three).

In conclusion, the conflict between the individual and society in "Fahrenheit 451" is a profound exploration of the human struggle for intellectual freedom and individuality in the face of societal conformity and oppression. Through Montag's journey, Bradbury illuminates the importance of critical thought and the courage to challenge the status quo. The novel serves as a stark reminder of the dangers of a society that stifles individuality and enforces homogeneity, underscoring the eternal value of dissent and diversity of thought.

Man vs. Technology

The conflict between man and technology in Bradbury's "Fahrenheit 451" is a significant theme that explores the complexities and dangers of technological advancement in a society that has become overly dependent on and controlled by technology. This conflict is illustrated through various elements in the novel, offering a critical perspective on the impact of technology on human life, thought, and behavior. Let's expand on this conflict:

The Mechanical Hound as a Symbol of Technological Domination:

- **Representation of State Control**: The Mechanical Hound is a key technological entity in the novel, representing the state's oppressive power. It is a tool of surveillance and enforcement used to track down and eliminate those who challenge the status quo. The Hound's existence and function exemplify the use of technology for control and suppression, illustrating a conflict between human freedom and technological domination.

- **Reference**: The description of the Hound: "It was like a great bee come home from the field" (Bradbury, Part One), depicts its mechanical precision and the threat it poses to Montag and others who seek knowledge.

The 'Parlor Walls' and Seashell Radios:

- **Technological Escapism and Isolation**: The 'parlor walls' and Seashell radios are technologies that create a sensory and information bubble, isolating individuals from reality and each other. They represent the conflict between human connection and the escapist allure of technology, which provides superficial entertainment and distraction, leading to a lack of genuine communication and understanding.

- **Reference**: Mildred's obsession with the 'parlor walls': "Now my 'family' is people. They tell me things; I laugh, they laugh!" (Bradbury, Part One) highlights her disconnection from real human interaction and her absorption in the artificial world created by technology.

Destruction of Books and Intellectualism:

- **Suppression of Knowledge Through Technology**: The systematic burning of books using technological means symbolizes the conflict between the pursuit of knowledge and the technological enforcement of ignorance. Firemen use advanced equipment to destroy books, a metaphor for the obliteration of intellectual freedom and critical thinking by technological means.

- **Reference**: Montag's realization of the destructive nature of his role: "We burned a thousand books. We burned a woman" (Bradbury, Part Two), emphasizes the conflict between his growing desire for knowledge and the technology-enforced censorship.

Technological Control vs. Human Rebellion:
- **Montag's Transformation**: Montag's journey from a fireman, a symbol of technological enforcement, to a rebel seeking freedom and truth, embodies the conflict between human agency and technological control. His rebellion represents a fight for human values in a society increasingly dominated by technology.

- **Reference**: Montag's theft of books and his eventual fleeing from the mechanical society reflect this human-versus-technology conflict: "He felt as if he had left a stage behind and many actors" (Bradbury, Part Three).

The Role of Technology in Society:
- **Critique of Overreliance on Technology**: The novel serves as an allegory for the dangers of an overreliance on technology at the expense of human qualities. It warns of a society where technology, rather than being a tool for human benefit, becomes a means of control, distraction, and dehumanization.

- **Reference**: Faber's discussion with Montag about the role of books and technology: "The magic is only in what books say ..." (Bradbury, Part Two), highlights the importance of human thought and interaction over technological dependency.

In conclusion, the conflict between man and technology in "Fahrenheit 451" is a profound exploration of the consequences of technological advancement when it surpasses and suppresses human values, freedom, and intellectualism. Bradbury presents a cautionary tale of a future where technology, rather than being an aid, becomes a tool for societal control and intellectual stagnation, urging readers to consider the importance of maintaining a balance between technological progress and the preservation of essential human qualities.

Individual vs. Self

The conflict of Individual vs. Self in "Fahrenheit 451" primarily manifests in the protagonist, Guy Montag, and his profound internal struggle. This conflict drives much of the narrative and is pivotal to the thematic exploration of the novel. Montag's journey of self-discovery and transformation reflects a broader commentary on identity, belief, and the human condition within a repressive society. Let's delve deeper into this internal conflict:

1. **Montag's Initial State of Contentment and Complacency**:

   ○ **Unquestioning Conformity**: Initially, Montag is depicted as a contented fireman, proud of his profession and its role in society. He is a product of his environment, unquestioningly conforming to societal norms and the government's anti-intellectual policies.

   ○ **Reference**: Montag's initial pride in his work: "It was a pleasure to burn" (Bradbury, Part One), signifies his initial alignment with societal values and his lack of self-awareness.

2. **Emergence of Doubt and Internal Conflict**:

   ○ **Encounter with Clarisse McClellan**: Montag's meetings with Clarisse mark the beginning of his internal struggle. Her questioning nature and appreciation of the world's simple joys starkly contrast with Montag's life, leading him to question his happiness and the society's norms.

○ **Reference**: Clarisse's simple question, "Are you happy?" (Bradbury, Part One), plants the seed of doubt in Montag's mind, triggering his introspective journey.

3. Montag's Growing Discontent and Self-Realization:

○ **Awareness of Societal Superficiality**: As Montag becomes more aware of the superficiality and oppressiveness of his society, particularly through his interactions with his wife Mildred and her friends, his internal conflict intensifies. He begins to feel isolated and disillusioned with the life he has been leading.

○ **Secret Rebellion Through Books**: Montag's decision to secretly collect and read books is a pivotal moment in his self-conflict. It signifies a shift from passive acceptance to active questioning of societal norms and his role in them.

○ **Reference**: The act of reading and questioning leads Montag to a realization: "He felt his body divide itself into a hotness and a coldness, a softness and a hardness, a trembling and a not trembling, the two halves grinding one upon the other" (Bradbury, Part Two).

4. Crisis of Identity and Morality:

○ **Struggle with Guilt and Fear**: Montag's growing empathy and understanding through literature bring him into moral conflict with his duties as a fireman. He experiences guilt over his past actions and fear of the consequences of his newfound rebellion.

- **Reference**: Montag's crisis reaches its peak during his confrontation with Beatty, where he is forced to confront the reality of his actions and the society he has been a part of: "We burned a thousand books. We burned a woman" (Bradbury, Part Two).

5. Resolution and Transformation:

- **Rejection of the Old Self**: The climax of Montag's internal struggle is his complete rejection of his former self, symbolized by his act of defiance against Captain Beatty and his escape from the city.

- **Joining the 'Book People'**: Montag's integration into the 'Book People' represents the resolution of his internal conflict. He finds purpose in preserving knowledge and embracing a new identity that values intellectual freedom and individual thought.

- **Reference**: Montag's reflection on his transformation: "He was not empty. There was more than enough here to fill him" (Bradbury, Part Three), signifies his acceptance of his new self.

In conclusion, the Individual vs. Self conflict in "Fahrenheit 451" is a compelling exploration of the human struggle for self-awareness and authenticity in a world that discourages individual thought and expression. Through Montag's internal journey, Bradbury highlights the importance of introspection, the courage to challenge one's beliefs, and the transformative power of knowledge. Montag's conflict and eventual resolution offer a message of hope and the affirmation of the individual's capacity for change and growth.

Individual vs. Authority

The conflict between the individual and authority in Ray Bradbury's "Fahrenheit 451" is a central theme that underscores the tension between personal freedom and state control. This conflict is vividly illustrated through the character of Guy Montag and his interactions with the figures of authority in the dystopian society, especially Captain Beatty. Let's delve deeper into the aspects of this conflict:

1. **Montag's Role as a Fireman**:

   ○ **Initial Alignment with Authority**: Montag begins the novel as a fireman, an agent of the authoritarian regime, enforcing the societal prohibition against books. His role embodies the government's oppressive control over knowledge and individual freedom.

   ○ **Reference**: Montag's pride in his work and adherence to state authority is evident early in the novel: "It was a pleasure to burn" (Bradbury, Part One), indicating his initial acceptance of and complicity with the authoritarian regime.

2. **The Firehouse as a Symbol of Authority**:

   ○ **Control and Conformity**: The firehouse, where Montag works, symbolizes the control exerted by the government over its citizens. It is a place of conformity, where firemen are indoctrinated to follow orders without question and suppress dissent or individual thought.

- ○ **Reference**: The mechanical hound stationed at the firehouse, a tool of state control and enforcement, represents this authority: "The Hound half rose in its kennel and looked at him with green-blue neon light flickering in its suddenly activated eye bulbs" (Bradbury, Part One).

3. **Captain Beatty as the Personification of Authority**:

- ○ **Intellectual Oppressor**: Captain Beatty, as Montag's superior and the fire chief, personifies the oppressive authority of the state. He is well-read and understands the power of literature, yet he uses his knowledge to justify the suppression of books and to manipulate Montag.

- ○ **Reference**: Beatty's speeches to Montag about the dangers of books and the necessity of censorship represent this authoritarian perspective: "We must all be alike. Not everyone born free and equal, as the Constitution says, but everyone made equal" (Bradbury, Part One).

4. **Montag's Growing Rebellion**:

- ○ **Questioning and Resistance**: Montag's encounters with Clarisse and his secret accumulation of books mark the beginning of his rebellion against the authority. He starts questioning the state's policies and his role in enforcing them, leading to a growing conflict with the authorities represented by the firehouse and Beatty.

- ○ **Reference**: Montag's internal conflict becomes external when he reads poetry to his wife and her friends, an act of defiance against the societal norms: "He read a dozen pages here or there and came at last to this: 'It was a pleasure to burn'" (Bradbury, Part Two).

5. **Climactic Confrontation and Resolution**:

- **Direct Conflict with Beatty**: The climax of Montag's conflict with authority occurs when he is forced to burn his own house and, in a moment of desperation, kills Beatty. This act signifies his complete rejection of the oppressive system and marks his final break from the role of a fireman.

- **Reference**: The confrontation between Montag and Beatty: "Montag only said, 'We never burned right...'" (Bradbury, Part Three), symbolizes his rebellion against the authoritarian regime.

In conclusion, the conflict between the individual and authority in "Fahrenheit 451" highlights the struggle for personal freedom and intellectual independence in the face of an oppressive regime. Through Montag's journey from conformity to rebellion, Bradbury explores the moral and ethical implications of state control and censorship. This conflict warns against the dangers of authoritarianism and underscores the importance of individual thought and resistance in maintaining a free and open society.

Society vs. Intellectualism

The conflict between society and intellectualism in "Fahrenheit 451" is a central theme that addresses the tension between societal conformity and the pursuit of knowledge and critical thinking. This conflict is woven throughout the narrative, reflecting Bradbury's concern about the potential consequences of a society that devalues intellectual pursuits in favor of homogeneity and superficiality. Let's expand on this conflict:

1. **Societal Anti-Intellectualism**:

   ○ **Enforced Ignorance**: The society depicted in "Fahrenheit 451" actively suppresses intellectualism, primarily by banning and burning books. This represents a deliberate attempt by the authorities to maintain control by keeping the populace ignorant and unthinking.

   ○ **Reference**: Captain Beatty's explanation of the society's history to Montag illustrates this enforced ignorance: "School is shortened, discipline relaxed, philosophies, histories, languages dropped, English and spelling gradually neglected, finally almost completely ignored" (Bradbury, Part One).

2. **Dichotomy Between Knowledge and Ignorance**:

   ○ **Suppression of Diverse Thought**: The society in the novel equates intellectualism with dissent and discomfort, seeing books and the diverse ideas they contain as a threat to social order and happiness.

○ **Reference**: Beatty's discussion about the danger of books reflects this dichotomy: "A book is a loaded gun in the house next door...Who knows who might be the target of the well-read man?" (Bradbury, Part One).

3. **The Role of Education and Media**:

○ **Shallow Education and Sensational Media**: The novel portrays a society where education is shallow and devoid of critical thought, and the media, represented by the 'parlor walls,' is used to disseminate superficial and sensational content.

○ **Reference**: Mildred's addiction to the 'parlor walls' and her disconnection from reality symbolize the societal preference for entertainment over intellectualism: "My 'family' is people. They tell me things; I laugh, they laugh!" (Bradbury, Part One).

4. **Individual Struggle Against Societal Norms**:

○ **Montag's Transformation**: Montag's journey from a fireman, a symbol of state suppression, to a seeker of knowledge, represents the individual struggle against anti-intellectual societal norms.

○ **Reference**: Montag's growing curiosity and his secret hoarding of books signify his resistance to societal norms: "He felt his body divide itself into a hotness and a coldness, a softness and a hardness, a trembling and a not trembling, the two halves grinding one upon the other" (Bradbury, Part Two).

5. Intellectual Resistance:

○ **The 'Book People'**: The group of individuals who memorize books, known as the 'Book People,' represents a form of intellectual resistance. They symbolize the preservation of knowledge and intellectualism in a society that seeks to eradicate it.

○ **Reference**: Granger and the 'Book People' demonstrate this resistance: "We're remembering" (Bradbury, Part Three).

6. Conclusion and Hope for Intellectualism:

○ **Resilience of Knowledge**: Despite the society's efforts to suppress intellectualism, the novel concludes with a note of hope that knowledge and intellectualism can endure and eventually prevail.

○ **Reference**: The novel's ending, with Montag and the 'Book People' contemplating the rebuilding of society after its destruction, suggests the resilience of intellectualism: "And when the war's over, some day, some year, the books can be written again..." (Bradbury, Part Three).

In conclusion, the conflict between society and intellectualism in "Fahrenheit 451" highlights the dangers of a society that chooses ignorance over knowledge and uniformity over diversity of thought. Through Montag's transformation and the existence of the 'Book People,' Bradbury emphasizes the importance of intellectualism and critical thinking as essential components of a free and vibrant society. The novel serves as a warning against the complacency and conformity that can lead to the suppression of intellectual freedom and encourages a commitment to preserving and celebrating knowledge.

CLIMAX

Ray Bradbury's "Fahrenheit 451" climax occurs in Part Three of the novel, titled "Burning Bright." This climactic section is filled with intense action and profound revelations that mark the peak of Guy Montag's transformation and his conflict with the dystopian society. The climax can be pinpointed to the confrontation between Montag and Captain Beatty at Montag's home. Here's a detailed exploration of this climactic moment:

1. **Montag's Home is Targeted**:

   ○ **Context**: The climax begins when the firemen, led by Captain Beatty, are called to an alarm that surprisingly leads them to Montag's own house. It is revealed that Montag's wife Mildred has betrayed him by reporting his possession of books.

   ○ **Reference**: "Montag, go home. Why waste your final hours racing about your cage denying you're a squirrel?" (Bradbury, Part Three), taunts Beatty, indicating Montag's imminent downfall.

2. **Beatty's Provocation and Montag's Defiance**:

   ○ **Montag's Forced Compliance**: Beatty forces Montag to burn his house with his flamethrower, symbolizing Montag's complete break with his past life and his role as a fireman.

   ○ **Reference**: "Burn it, Montag! Pour the kerosene!" (Bradbury,

Part Three), Beatty commands, compelling Montag to destroy his own sanctuary of knowledge.

3. Discovery of the Earpiece:

- **Beatty's Discovery**: As Montag burns his house, Beatty discovers the earpiece through which Montag has been communicating with Faber. Beatty plans to trace it back to Faber, threatening to destroy another remnant of intellectualism.

- **Reference**: "And I thought you were the one. I thought you were the one who had been shaken up," (Bradbury, Part Three), Beatty sneers, revealing his knowledge of Montag's connection to Faber.

4. Montag's Rebellion and Beatty's Death:

- **Turning Point**: In a moment of intense emotion and realization, Montag turns the flamethrower on Beatty and kills him. This act represents Montag's final rebellion against the oppressive society and the authoritative figure of Beatty.

- **Reference**: "Beatty, he thought, you're not a problem now. You always said, don't face a problem, burn it. Well, now I've done both. Goodbye, Captain" (Bradbury, Part Three), reflects Montag's resolution and the significance of his actions.

5. Montag's Escape:

- **Fleeing the Scene**: After killing Beatty, Montag is forced to flee as the Mechanical Hound attacks him. He manages to escape, injured but alive, marking his physical and symbolic departure from the oppressive society.

- ○ **Reference**: "He stumbled towards the bed and shoved the book clumsily under the cold pillow. He fell into bed, and his wife cried out, startled. He lay far across the room from her, on a winter island separated by an empty sea" (Bradbury, Part Three), which symbolizes Montag's final separation from his old life.

6. **Montag's Transformation Complete**:

- ○ **Resolution of Internal Conflict**: The climax resolves Montag's internal conflict. His act of defiance solidifies his transformation from a conformist fireman to a free-thinking individual, willing to take drastic actions for his beliefs.

- ○ **Reference**: "He felt as if he had left a stage behind and many actors. He felt as if he had left the great séance and all the murmuring ghosts. He was moving from an unreality that was frightening into a reality that was unreal because it was new" (Bradbury, Part Three); Montag reflects on his newfound freedom.

In conclusion, the climax of "Fahrenheit 451" is a moment of intense action and emotional release. It represents the culmination of Montag's struggle against the oppressive society and his own personal transformation. This climactic event propels Montag into a new phase of his life and encapsulates the novel's central themes of rebellion, the pursuit of knowledge, and the fight against censorship.

RESOLUTION

Ray Bradbury's "Fahrenheit 451" resolution follows the climactic confrontation between Montag and Captain Beatty and Montag's subsequent escape from the city. This resolution phase, which occupies the latter part of the novel, brings closure to Montag's personal journey and leaves the reader with a contemplative vision of hope and rebirth amidst destruction. Here's a detailed exploration of the resolution:

1. **Montag's Flight and Encounter with the 'Book People'**:

    ○ **Escape from the City**: Montag flees the city after the dramatic climax of killing Beatty and escaping the Mechanical Hound. He finds refuge in the natural environment outside the city, which starkly contrasts with the oppressive urban setting he leaves behind.

    ○ **Reference**: "He was three hundred yards downstream when the Hound reached the river" (Bradbury, Part Three), describes Montag's narrow escape and his transition to a different world.

2. **Meeting Granger and the 'Book People'**:

    ○ **Introduction to a New Community**: Montag encounters a group of exiles living outside the city, known as the 'Book People.' Led by Granger, they are committed to preserving literary knowledge by memorizing books, each person taking responsibility for a different piece of literature.

- ○ **Reference**: "We're book burners, too. We read the books and burnt them, afraid they'd be found. Microfilming didn't pay off; we were always traveling, we didn't want to bury the film and come back later. Always the chance of discovery. Better to keep it in the old heads, where no one can see it or suspect it" (Bradbury, Part Three); Granger explains their mission.

3. **Montag's Integration and New Purpose**:

- ○ **Acceptance into the Group**: Montag finds a sense of belonging and purpose with the 'Book People.' He learns about their mission to preserve knowledge in an age of ignorance, and he becomes part of their efforts, taking on the responsibility of remembering a book.

- ○ **Reference**: "You're welcome," said Granger. "You'll be alright" (Bradbury, Part Three), signifies Montag's acceptance into the group and his new role in preserving knowledge.

4. **Destruction and Renewal**:

- ○ **Destruction of the City**: The novel ends with the distant destruction of the city by bombs, likely in a war that has been hinted at throughout the narrative. This destruction symbolizes the ultimate consequence of the society's ignorance and conformity.

- ○ **Reference**: "A long time ago, a man named Plato said that he was not himself when he was awake, he was only truly himself when he was asleep" (Bradbury, Part Three), an allusion that suggests a new beginning from the ashes of the old.

5. **Hope for the Future**:

- ○ **Prospects of Rebirth and Knowledge**: The novel concludes with Montag and the 'Book People' preparing to return to the ruined city with the hope of rebuilding society. This resolution offers a message of hope and the enduring power of human knowledge and resilience.

- ○ **Reference**: "And when the war's over, some day, some year, the books can be written again..." (Bradbury, Part Three), Granger muses, indicating the potential for rebirth and a new, more enlightened society.

In conclusion, the resolution of "Fahrenheit 451" provides a somber yet hopeful ending to Montag's story. It shows the protagonist finding a new community and purpose outside the confines of the oppressive society he has left. The novel closes with the idea that there is an opportunity for rebirth and change even in the wake of destruction. Bradbury leaves readers with a reflective vision of the future, emphasizing the importance of memory, knowledge, and the resilience of the human spirit.

Morals of the Story

"Fahrenheit 451" is abundant with moral lessons that resonate with readers regarding the importance of intellectual freedom, the dangers of censorship, and the value of individual thought. Here are some key morals of the story, supported by references from the novel:

1. **The Dangers of Censorship and Conformity**:

   - **Moral**: Censorship suppresses individual thought and leads to a stagnant, oppressive society. Conformity stifles creativity and intellectual growth, especially when enforced by an authority.

   - **Reference**: Captain Beatty explains to Montag, "Colored people don't like Little Black Sambo. Burn it. White people don't feel good about Uncle Tom's Cabin. Burn it" (Bradbury, Part One). This highlights how censorship eliminates dissent and maintains a false sense of harmony.

2. **The Value of Knowledge and Literature**:

   - **Moral**: Knowledge and literature are fundamental to understanding the human experience and should be preserved. They foster empathy, critical thinking, and awareness of the world.

   - **Reference**: Faber tells Montag, "The magic is only in what books say, how they stitched the patches of the universe together into one garment for us" (Bradbury, Part Two), emphasizing the importance of literature in understanding and connecting with the world.

3. The Importance of Individual Thought and Questioning:

- **Moral**: Blind acceptance of societal norms leads to the loss of individuality and critical thinking. Questioning and challenging these norms to maintain a free and thoughtful society is important.

- **Reference**: Clarisse's question to Montag, "Are you happy?" (Bradbury, Part One), sparks his journey of self-questioning and rebellion against societal conformity.

4. The Negative Impact of Technology on Social Interaction:

- **Moral**: Over-reliance on technology can lead to a disconnected, superficial society where artificial and transient experiences replace genuine human interactions.

- **Reference**: Mildred's obsession with her 'family' in the 'parlor walls' and her disconnection from Montag illustrates the moral decay resulting from technology replacing real human relationships: "My 'family' is people. They tell me things; I laugh, they laugh!" (Bradbury, Part One).

5. The Power of Resistance and Hope:

- **Moral**: Resistance against oppressive forces, even when daunting, is vital. There is always hope for change and renewal, even in the darkest of times.

- **Reference**: The existence of the 'Book People' and their commitment to preserving knowledge signifies hope for a future where truth and freedom can flourish: "And when the war's over, some day, some year, the books can be written again..." (Bradbury, Part Three).

6. The Need for Reflection and Self-Awareness:

- **Moral**: Self-awareness and introspection are crucial for personal growth and understanding one's place in the world.

- **Reference**: Montag's reflection, "He was not empty. There was more than enough here to fill him" (Bradbury, Part Three), after meeting Granger and the 'Book People', signifies his realization of his new purpose and identity.

In conclusion, "Fahrenheit 451" presents several morals centered around the value of intellectual freedom, the perils of censorship, the importance of individual thought, the impact of technology on society, the power of resistance, and the need for personal reflection. These lessons are woven throughout the narrative, making the novel a compelling story and a profound commentary on the human condition.

MEMORABLE QUOTES

"Fahrenheit 451" is filled with memorable quotes that capture the essence of its themes and characters. These quotes have resonated with readers and are often cited for their insight into society, human nature, and the value of knowledge. Here are some of the most memorable quotes from the novel:

1. **On the Power and Joy of Burning Books**:

   - "It was a pleasure to burn."

   - **Context**: This opening line succinctly introduces the novel's central theme of destruction and censorship.

2. **On Individuality and Nonconformity**:

   - "If you hide your ignorance, no one will hit you and you'll never learn."

   - Context: Faber's words to Montag emphasize the importance of acknowledging one's ignorance as a step towards learning and personal growth.

3. **On the Importance of Books and Knowledge**:

   - "A book is a loaded gun in the house next door...Who knows who might be the target of the well-read man?"

   - Context: Captain Beatty's metaphorical statement to Montag highlights the perceived threat of books and the knowledge they contain.

4. **On the Role of Firemen in Society**:

○ "We burn them to ashes and then burn the ashes. That's our official motto."

○ **Context**: This line reveals the extent of the societal commitment to censorship and the erasure of dissenting ideas.

5. **On the Destructive Impact of Television**:

○ "'My 'family' is people. They tell me things; I laugh, they laugh!' And the colors!"

○ Context: Mildred's description of her interaction with the 'parlor walls' reflects the shallow, artificial nature of the entertainment that has replaced genuine human relationships.

6. **On the Escalation of Conflict and War**:

○ "It's always someone else's fault...you must remember that."

○ **Context**: This quote reflects the societal tendency to shift blame and avoid personal responsibility, a theme that underpins the novel's critique of a complacent and disconnected society.

7. **On Memory and Permanence**:

○ "Everyone must leave something behind when he dies... A child or a book or a painting or a house or a wall built or a pair of shoes made."

- ○ Context: Granger's reflections on the importance of leaving a legacy and contributing to the world emphasize the value of individual impact.

8. **On Hope and Rebirth**:

- ○ "And when he died, I suddenly realized I wasn't crying for him at all, but for all the things he did. I cried because he would never do them again."

- ○ **Context**: Montag's realization about the finality of death and the value of an individual's actions and experiences.

These quotes from "Fahrenheit 451" are central to understanding the novel's themes and offer profound insights into broader issues relevant to society, both in Bradbury's time and today. They underscore the dangers of censorship, the importance of critical thinking, and the enduring value of knowledge and individual action.